"I immediately went to my nurse man[...] NCLEX® and she referred me to ATI. [...] areas I was weak in, and focused on those areas in the review modules and online assessments.

I was much more prepared the second time around!"

Terim Richards
Nursing student

Danielle Platt

Nurse Manager • Children's Mercy Hospital • Kansas City, MO

"The year our hospital did not use the ATI program, we experienced a 15% decrease in the NCLEX® pass rates. We reinstated the ATI program the following year and had a 90% success rate."

"As a manager, I have witnessed graduate nurses fail the NCLEX® and the devastating effects it has on their morale. Once the nurses started using ATI, it was amazing to see the confidence they had in themselves and their ability to go forward and take the NCLEX® exam."

Mary Moss

Associate Dean of Nursing - Service and Health Division • Mid-State Technical College • Wisconsin Rapids, WI

"I like that ATI lets students know what to expect from the NCLEX®, helps them plan their study time and tells them what to do in the days and weeks before the exam. It is different from most of the NCLEX® review books on the market."

Editor

Jeanne Wissmann, PhD, RN, CNE
Director Nursing Curriculum and Educational Services
Assessment Technologies Institute®, LLC

Associate Editors

Audrey Knippa, MS, MPH, RN, CNE
Curriculum Project Coordinator

Derek Prater, MS Journalism
Product Developer

Copyright Notice

Important Notice to the Reader of this Publication

Preface

Overview

The overall goal of this Assessment Technologies Institute®, LLC (ATI) review module is to provide nursing students with an additional resource for the review and/or remediation of "Community Health" content relevant to entry level nursing practice. Content within this review module is provided in a key point plus rationale format in order to focus recall and application of relevant content. Chapter selections are reflective of the ATI "Community Health for Nursing Practice" assessment test plans and standard nursing curricular content. Each chapter begins with a set of learning objectives in an effort to guide the learner's review and application of chapter content.

Contributors

ATI would like to extend appreciation to the nurse educators and nurse specialists who contributed content for this review module. The names of contributors are noted in the chapter bylines. We would also like to thank those talented individuals who reviewed, edited, and developed this module. Additionally, we want to recognize and express appreciation to all of the contributors, reviewers, production developers, and editors of previous editions of this review module.

Suggestions for Effective Utilization

Δ   Some suggested uses of this review module include:

- As a review of community health-relevant content in developing and assessing readiness for entry level community health nursing practice.

- As a remediation resource based on the results of an ATI "Community Health for Nursing Practice" assessment. "Topics to Review" for these assessments will guide learners to chapters within this review module.

Δ   To foster long-term recall and development of an ability to apply knowledge to a variety of situations, learners are encouraged to take a comprehensive approach to topic review. Using this review module along with other resources (class notes, course textbooks, nursing reference texts, instructors, ATI DVD series), consider exploration of the topic, addressing questions such as:

- What are the nursing implications of "community" as a "client"?

- How do nurses provide "population-focused" nursing care?

- How do community-oriented and community-based nursing practice compare? Community health and public health nursing?

- What is the community health nurse's role in health promotion and disease prevention? In primary, secondary, and tertiary levels of prevention?

- How does *Healthy People 2010* guide community health nursing practice? What specific directives are given?

- How does the community health nurse use epidemiology in community health practice?

- What are the components of the epidemiological triangle and steps used in the epidemiological process?

- How does the community health nurse utilize proportion and ratios to determine disease incidence or prevalence, mortality rates, or attack rates?

- How is ethics a key function of community health nursing? What are client rights? What are the ethical decision-making processes utilized?

- How does the community health nurse serve as a client advocate?

- Why is it important that the community health nurse develops cultural awareness and cultural competence?

- What are the components of a cultural assessment? What are some examples of culturally sensitive interventions?

- What is the role of the community health nurse in community health education? What are different learning styles or possible barriers to learning and how should health education plans be modified accordingly?

- How does the community health nurse design a community health education plan based on an identified population-specific learning need?

- What is the role of community assessments in the identification of community needs, problems, strengths, and resources? What data should be collected by community assessments and what are appropriate methods for data collection?

- What are the phases involved in community health program planning and the role of the community health nurse in each phase? What are strategies and barriers for implementation of community health programs?

- What are the roles and responsibilities of the community health nurse in making referrals?

- What are barriers to health care access and what is the role of the community health nurse in assessing and ensuring accessibility of health care services?

- What are the roles of international, federal, state, and local health organizations in the promotion of the health of populations?

- What are financing options for the provision of community health resources?

- What are the roles and functions of home health, hospice, occupational health, school, and parish nurses and case managers?

- What are the health concerns/leading causes of death, screening/preventive services, *Healthy People 2010* initiatives, and community education foci in caring for community aggregates of children and adolescents? For women? For men? For older adults?

- What is the role of the community health nurse in the assessment and promotion of the health of families within a community and the *Healthy People 2010* initiatives related to family health?

- What is the community health nurse's role in meeting special community needs, including violence and abuse, substance abuse, mental illness, and homelessness?

- What is the community health nurse's role in promoting health in rural and migrant populations? Environmental health? Surveillance and reporting of infectious diseases? Promoting and providing immunizations? Communicable disease control?

- What is the role of the community health nurse in disaster planning and management, specifically in the disaster management phases of preparedness, response, and recovery? In preparing for and responding to bioterrorism?

Δ   Complete application exercises at the end of each chapter after a review of the topic. Answer questions fully and note rationales for answers. Complete exercises initially without looking for the answers within the chapter or consulting the answer key. Use these exercises as an opportunity to assess your readiness to apply knowledge. When reviewing the answer key, in addition to identifying the correct answer, examine why you missed or answered correctly each item—was it related to ability to recall, recognition of a common testing principle, or attention to key words?

Feedback

All feedback is welcome – suggestions for improvement, reports of mistakes (small or large), and testimonials of effectiveness. Please address feedback to: comments@atitesting.com

Table of Contents

Chapter 1:   Modes of Community Health Nursing
Contributor: Patricia Thompson, PhD, MSPH, RN

 Learning Objectives:

Δ   Discuss the concept of "community" as a "client" and as a "setting for practice."

Δ   Discuss population-focused nursing practice.

Δ   Compare and contrast community-oriented and community-based nursing practice.

Δ   Compare and contrast community health and public health nursing.

 Key Points

Δ   A community is a group of people and institutions that share geographic, civic, and/or social parameters.

Δ   Communities vary in their characteristics and health needs.

Δ   A community's health is determined by the degree to which the community's collective health needs are identified and met.

Δ   Health indicators (e.g., mortality rates, disease prevalence, levels of physical activity, obesity, tobacco use, substance abuse) are often used to describe the health status of a community and serve as targets for the improvement of a community's health.

Δ   Community health nurses are nurses who practice in the community. They usually have a facility from which they work (e.g., community health clinic, county health department), but their practice is not limited to institutional settings.

Δ   The community or a population (an aggregate who shares one or more personal characteristics) within the community is the "client" in community health nursing.

Δ   Community partnership occurs when the community actively participates in the processes for health promotion and disease prevention within the community. The development of community partnerships is critical to the accomplishment of health promotion and disease prevention strategies.

Δ   In population-focused nursing, assessments are made of and interventions are provided for defined "at risk" populations (e.g., individuals with hypertension, individuals with nutrition and weight problems).

	Focus of Care	Nursing Activities	Level of Preparation
Community-Oriented Nursing	Health of the community as a "whole" **Client:** Community	Health care: Surveillance and evaluation of the community's collective health	Generalist (e.g., Bachelor of Science in Nursing) or specialist (e.g., Master's degree in Community or Public Health Nursing)
Community-Based Nursing	Health of individuals, families, and groups within a community **Client:** Individual, family, or group of individuals	Illness care: Provision of direct primary care in the settings where individuals and families live, work, and "attend" (e.g., schools, camps, parishes)	Generalist (e.g., Bachelor of Science in Nursing) or specialist (e.g., Master's degree in Maternal-Infant Nursing, Pediatric Nursing, Adult Nursing, Mental Health Nursing)

	Theory Base	Goals and Functions
Community Health Nursing Practice	Synthesis of nursing and public health theory	Promote, preserve, and maintain the health of populations by the delivery of health services to individuals, families, and groups in order to impact "community health."
Public Health Nursing Practice	Synthesis of nursing and public health theory	Promote, preserve, and maintain the health of populations through disease and disability prevention and health protection of the community as a "whole." Core functions are 1) systematic assessment of the health of populations; 2) development of policies to support the health of populations; and 3) ensuring that essential health services are available to all persons.

Primary Reference:

Stanhope, M., & Lancaster, J. (2006). *Foundations of nursing in the community: Community-oriented practice* (2nd ed.). St. Louis, MO: Mosby.

Chapter 1: Modes of Community Health Nursing

Application Exercises

1. Which of the following is the fundamental factor that distinguishes public health nursing from other specialties?

   A. Focus on competence in nursing practice

   B. Population-focused practice

   C. Educational preparation and individual/family-focused practice

   D. Episodic care

2. Which of the following is the mode of community practice that is "setting-specific"?

   A. Community-oriented nursing practice

   B. Public health nursing practice

   C. Community health nursing practice

   D. Community-based nursing practice

Scenario: A community health nurse is working in a city of 200,000 residents. Adolescents in this city attend one of two high schools. Major problems for the adolescents in this town include tobacco use, depression, and teenage pregnancy. The nurse recognizes the need for health education for this aggregate. For the first health education project, she decides to partner with the local women's health clinic to provide education about prevention of teenage pregnancy.

---

3. Who is the community?

4. Who is the population?

5. How would the practice of a community health nurse fit in this situation?

Chapter 1: Modes of Community Health Nursing

Application Exercises Answer Key

1. Which of the following is the fundamental factor that distinguishes public health nursing from other specialties?

   A. Focus on competence in nursing practice

   B. Population-focused practice

   C. Educational preparation and individual/family-focused practice

   D. Episodic care

   The focus in public health nursing is to promote, preserve, and maintain the health of populations through disease and disability prevention and protection of the health of the community as a "whole."

2. Which of the following is the mode of community practice that is "setting-specific"?

   A. Community-oriented nursing practice

   B. Public health nursing practice

   C. Community health nursing practice

   D. Community-based nursing practice

   Community-based nursing practice involves the provision of direct primary care (acute and chronic) in the settings where individuals and families live, work, and "attend" (e.g., schools, camps, parishes).

Scenario: A community health nurse is working in a city of 200,000 residents. Adolescents in this city attend one of two high schools. Major problems for the adolescents in this town include tobacco use, depression, and teenage pregnancy. The nurse recognizes the need for health education for this aggregate. For the first health education project, she decides to partner with the local women's health clinic to provide education about prevention of teenage pregnancy.

3. Who is the community?

The city is the community. A community is a group of people with something in common who interact with each other and may share a goal or geographic boundary.

4. Who is the population?

The adolescents in this city are the population. A population is a group of people that have at least one thing in common, but they may not interact with each other.

5. How would the practice of a community health nurse fit in this situation?

The practice of a community health nurse is applicable to this situation. Community health nurses synthesize nursing and public health practice to promote and preserve the health of the population. A major responsibility of the nurse is health promotion and disease prevention, which the nurse is accomplishing by implementing a program to prevent teenage pregnancy. The nurse is also demonstrating the importance of developing partnerships within the community by working with the local women's health clinic to coordinate education. The population of adolescents in this city is the client in this setting, which is consistent with the practice of community health nursing, where the client is not an individual but a group of people.

Chapter 2:	Health Promotion and Disease Prevention

Contributor: Patricia Thompson, PhD, MSPH, RN

 Learning Objectives:

Δ Describe the community health nurse's role in health promotion and disease prevention.

Δ Discuss and differentiate between primary, secondary, and tertiary levels of prevention.

Δ Discuss *Healthy People 2010*.

Δ Describe the role of the community health nurse in health screening (secondary prevention).

 Key Points

Δ Health promotion involves strategies to improve individual and community health.

Δ The community health nurse actively helps people to change their lifestyles in order to move toward a state of optimal health (physical and psychosocial health).

Δ Preventive services include health education and counseling, immunizations, and other actions that aim to prevent a potential disease or disability.

Δ The community health nurse provides preventive services in multiple community settings.

Δ The community health nurse is often responsible for planning and implementing screening programs for at-risk populations.

Δ Successful screening programs provide accurate, reliable results, can be inexpensively and quickly administered to large groups, and produce few, if any, side effects.

Levels of Disease Prevention	Examples of Community Health Nurse Prevention Activities
Primary Prevention **Focus:** Prevention of the initial occurrence of disease or injury	• Nutrition counseling • Family planning and sex education • Smoking cessation education • Education about communicable diseases • Education about health and hygiene issues to specific groups (e.g., day care workers, restaurant workers) • Safety education (e.g., seatbelt use, helmet use) • Prenatal classes • Providing immunizations • Community assessments • Disease surveillance (communicable diseases) • Advocating for the resolution of health issues (e.g., access to health care, healthy environments)
Secondary Prevention **Focus:** Early detection of disease and treatment with the goal of limiting severity and adverse effects	• Screenings ◊ Cancer (breast, cervical, testicular, prostate, colorectal) ◊ Diabetes mellitus ◊ Hypertension ◊ Hypercholesterolemia ◊ Sensory impairments ◊ Tuberculosis ◊ Lead exposure ◊ Genetic disorders/metabolic deficiencies in newborns • Treatment of sexually transmitted diseases • Treatment of tuberculosis • Control of outbreaks of communicable diseases
Tertiary Prevention **Focus:** Maximization of recovery after an injury or illness (rehabilitation)	• Nutrition counseling • Exercise rehabilitation • Case management (chronic illness, mental illness) • Shelters • Support groups • Exercise for hypertensive clients (individual)

Healthy People 2010

Δ   *Healthy People 2010* is the third 10-year plan for the health of the United States. Managed by the U.S. Department of Health and Human Services' Office of Disease Prevention and Health Promotion, it builds on both *Healthy People* and *Healthy People 2000*. *Healthy People 2010* has 28 areas of focus with 467 objectives. This document is built on a systematic approach using four elements: goals, objectives, determinants of health, and health status. The focus is on promoting healthy behaviors, promoting safe and healthy communities, and improving systems for public and individual health. The document stresses that all Americans can help to attain these goals.

Δ   **Healthy People 2010 has two central goals for the health of Americans:**

- Increase quality and years of healthy life.

- Eliminate health disparities.

Δ   *Healthy People 2010* established a list of **leading health indicators** to help communities and individuals target areas for improving the health of both the individual and the community. These indicators are behaviors, physical and social environmental factors, and health system issues that affect the health of communities and individuals. The leading health indicators are:

- Physical activity.

- Overweight and obesity.

- Tobacco use.

- Substance abuse.

- Responsible sexual behavior.

- Mental health.

- Injury and violence.

- Environmental quality.

- Immunizations.

- Access to health care.

Δ   **Healthy People 2010 Focus Areas**

- Access to quality health services

- Arthritis, osteoporosis, and chronic back conditions

- Cancer

- Chronic kidney disease

- Diabetes mellitus

- Disability and secondary conditions

- Educational and community-based programs

- Environmental health

- Family planning

- Food safety

- Health communication

- Heart disease and stroke

- Human immunodeficiency virus (HIV)

- Immunization and infectious diseases

- Injury and violence prevention

- Maternal, infant, and child health

- Medical product safety

- Mental health and mental disorders

- Nutrition and weight regulation

- Occupational safety and health

- Oral health

- Physical activity and fitness

- Public health infrastructure

- Respiratory disease

- Sexually transmitted disease

- Substance abuse

- Tobacco use

- Vision and hearing

Δ   The community health nurse should be familiar with the objectives of *Healthy People 2010* and committed to meeting these national health care objectives.

Primary Reference:

Stanhope, M., & Lancaster, J. (2006). *Foundations of nursing in the community: Community-oriented practice* (2nd ed.). St. Louis, MO: Mosby.

Additional Resources:

Centers for Disease Control and Prevention. (n.d.). *Preventing lead poisoning in young children.* Retrieved on March 5, 2007, from http://www.cdc.gov/nceh/lead/publications/books/plpyc/chapter4.htm#Anticipatory%20Guidance

U.S. Department of Health and Human Services. (n.d.). *Healthy People 2010.* Retrieved February 15, 2007, from http://www.healthypeople.gov/

Chapter 2: Health Promotion and Disease Prevention

Application Exercises

1. Match the following community health nursing activities with the appropriate level of prevention.

   _____ Diabetic foot screenings   A. Primary

   _____ Infant immunizations   B. Secondary

   _____ Cardiac rehabilitation program   C. Tertiary

Scenario: A community health nurse is assisting the county in completing a community assessment. He is working with the county board of supervisors to determine funding for programs for the next year. Significant problems discovered during the assessment include: identification of an unsafe intersection, need for improvement in the playground equipment at several parks, a high rate of substance abuse, a high rate of lead poisoning in young children, and an infant mortality rate that is higher than the national average.

---

2. Using *Healthy People 2010* as a guide, which of the indicated health issues should receive priority for funding?

3. The community health nurse secures funding for a lead screening program to be conducted in the county. What activities can the nurse implement?

4. For each of the following topics, identify an intervention that is appropriate for the identified client focus and level of prevention.

Topic	Focus Area	Level of Prevention	Intervention
Teenage pregnancy	Individual	Primary	
Scoliosis	Group	Secondary	
Stroke	Individual	Tertiary	
Breast cancer	Community	Secondary	
Seat-belt usage	Community	Primary	
School violence	Group	Tertiary	
Vaccinations	Individual	Primary	
STDs	Group	Secondary	
Homelessness	Community	Tertiary	

Chapter 2: Health Promotion and Disease Prevention

Application Exercises Answer Key

1. Match the following community health nursing activities with the appropriate level of prevention.

B   Diabetic foot screenings   A. Primary

A   Infant immunizations   B. Secondary

C   Cardiac rehabilitation program   C. Tertiary

Screenings are secondary prevention measures for the early detection of disease. Immunizations are primary prevention measures to prevent the development of diseases. Rehabilitation is the major focus of tertiary prevention measures.

Scenario: A community health nurse is assisting the county in completing a community assessment. He is working with the county board of supervisors to determine funding for programs for the next year. Significant problems discovered during the assessment include: identification of an unsafe intersection, need for improvement in the playground equipment at several parks, a high rate of substance abuse, a high rate of lead poisoning in young children, and an infant mortality rate that is higher than the national average.

---

2. Using *Healthy People 2010* as a guide, which of the indicated health issues should receive priority for funding?

All of the identified problems are included in *Healthy People 2010*'s 28 focus areas:

> **Identification of an unsafe intersection (injury and violence prevention)**
> **Need for improvement in the playground equipment (injury and violence prevention)**
> **High rate of substance abuse (substance abuse)**
> **High rate of lead poisoning in young children (environmental health)**
> **Infant mortality rate higher than the national average (maternal, infant, and child health)**

3. The community health nurse secures funding for a lead screening program to be conducted in the county. What activities can the nurse implement?

The community health nurse can assist with coordinating a free lead-screening clinic for children. Guidelines for testing can be obtained from the CDC or from a state agency involved with lead poisoning prevention. The clinic should be followed with education for parents in the community to include: implications of results of lead screening and need for further testing, anticipatory guidance regarding sources of lead poisoning and ways to prevent exposure, resources for safe removal of lead-based paint from their homes, housekeeping measures to reduce exposure to dust (e.g., wet mopping floors, window sills, and other hard surfaces with high-phosphate solutions in houses built before 1960), and the importance of using good handwashing techniques, washing toys and pacifiers frequently, and good nutrition (regular meals with adequate iron and calcium in the diet).

4. For each of the following topics, identify an intervention that is appropriate for the identified client focus and level of prevention.

Topic	Focus Area	Level of Prevention	Intervention
Teenage pregnancy	Individual	Primary	**Education about prevention of teenage pregnancy to an 8th-grade student at a school-based clinic**
Scoliosis	Group	Secondary	**Providing scoliosis screening in a middle school**
Stroke	Individual	Tertiary	**Performing range-of-motion exercises with a client following a stroke**
Breast cancer	Community	Secondary	**Using TV to advertise a breast cancer screening program**
Seat-belt usage	Community	Primary	**Promoting use of a billboard ad: "Buckle Up for Safety"**
School violence	Group	Tertiary	**Hosting a PTA presentation about school safety at a school following an incident where a student brought a knife to school**
Vaccinations	Individual	Primary	**Administering an MMR vaccination to a 12-month-old infant**
STDs	Group	Secondary	**Providing free STD screening to students on a college campus**
Homelessness	Community	Tertiary	**Assisting the Salvation Army in fundraising to build a new women's shelter for the homeless population in the community**

Chapter 3: Epidemiological Perspective
Contributor: Carel Mountain, MSN, RN

 Learning Objectives:

Δ   Discuss the role of epidemiology in community health and how nurses use epidemiology in community health practice.

Δ   Discuss the epidemiological triangle and the steps used in the epidemiological process.

Δ   Use proportion and ratios to determine disease incidence or prevalence, mortality rates, and attack rates.

 Key Points

Δ   Epidemiology is the investigative study of disease trends in populations for the purposes of disease prevention and health maintenance. Epidemiology relies on statistical evidence to determine the rate of spread of disease and the proportion of people affected by that disease. It also is used to evaluate the effectiveness of disease prevention and health promotion activities and to determine the extent to which goals of health promotion and disease prevention initiatives (e.g., *Healthy People 2010*) have been met.

Δ   Epidemiology is useful for community-based nursing in providing a broad understanding of the spread and transmission of disease. This information often forms the basis of community health presentations. Using the scientific problem-solving method, the nurse is able to pinpoint health needs in the community and develop appropriate approaches. Community health nurses are in the unique position of being able to identify cases, recognize patterns of disease, eliminate barriers to disease control, and provide education and counseling targeted at a disease condition or specific risk factors.

Δ   Epidemiology involves the study of the relationships among an agent, a host, and an environment (referred to as the **epidemiological triangle**). Their interaction determines the development and cessation of communicable diseases, and they form a web of causality, which increases or decreases the risk for disease.

•   The **agent** is the animate or inanimate object that causes the disease.

•   The **host** is the living being that will be affected by the agent.

•   The **environment** is the setting or surrounding that sustains the host.

Epidemiological Triangle

Susceptible Individuals (Hosts)

- Altered immunity
- Altered resistance
- Risk characteristics
  - ◊ Genetics
  - ◊ Gender
  - ◊ Age
  - ◊ Physiological state
  - ◊ Prior disease state
  - ◊ Social class
  - ◊ Cultural group
  - ◊ Occupation

Not Susceptible Individuals (Hosts)

- Active immunity
  - ◊ Natural
  - ◊ Artificial
- Passive immunity
  - ◊ Natural
  - ◊ Artificial

Vehicle (nonliving) Vectors

- Clothing
- Food
- Water

Intermediary (living) Vectors

- Mosquitios
- Fleas
- Rodents
- Birds

Infectious Agents

- Viruses
- Fungi
- Bacteria

Physical Agents

- Trauma
- Genetics
- Noise
- Temperature

Chemical Agents

- Drugs
- Fumes
- Toxins

Environmental Reservoirs and Modes of Transmission

- Human resevoirs
- Physical factors
- Temperature
- Rainfall
- Socioeconomic factors
- Availability of resources
- Access to health care
- High-risk working conditions
- Crowded living conditions

Epidemiological Process

Determine the nature, extent, and possible significance of the problem.	During this phase of the process, the nurse collects information from as many sources as possible. This information is then used to determine the scope of the problem.
Utilizing the gathered data, formulate a possible theory.	At this time, the possible explanations are projected and explored for consideration.
Gather information from a variety of sources in order to narrow down the possibilities.	Assess all possible sites for the amassing of information related to the disease process. Evaluate the plausibility of the proposed hypothesis.
Make the plan.	In this phase of the process, the nurse focuses on breaking the cycle of disease. All factors influencing the spread of the disease must be considered and identified. Priorities are established to break the chain of transmission and to control the spread of the disease.
Put the plan into action.	Using all available means, the plan for controlling the disease is put into action.
Evaluate the plan.	Gather pertinent information to determine the success of the plan. Using this plan, evaluate the success in prevention of the spread of the disease.
Report and follow up.	Synthesize evaluation data into a format that is understandable. Evaluate successes and failures and base follow-up on the evaluation information.

Epidemiological Calculations

Δ   **Incidence** (new cases)

$$\frac{\text{\# of Cases Detected}}{\text{Population Total}} \times 1{,}000 = \underline{\hspace{2cm}} \text{ per 1,000}$$

Δ   **Prevalence** (existing disease in a population at a particular time)

$$\frac{\text{\# of Cases in the Population at a Specific Time}}{\text{Population Total}} \times 1{,}000 = \underline{\hspace{2cm}} \text{ per 1,000}$$

Δ   **Mortality Rates**

$$\frac{\text{\# of Deaths}}{\text{Population Total}} \times 1{,}000 = \underline{\hspace{2cm}} \text{ per 1,000}$$

Δ   **Attack Rates**

$$\frac{\text{\# of People at Risk Who Develop a Certain Disease}}{\text{Total \# of People at Risk}}$$

Δ   An **epidemic** is when the rate of disease exceeds the usual level of the condition.

Primary Reference:

Stanhope, M., & Lancaster, J. (2006). *Foundations of nursing in the community: Community-oriented practice* (2nd ed.). St. Louis, MO: Mosby.

Chapter 3: Epidemiological Perspective

Application Exercises

Scenario: A client presents with measles.

1. Who/what is the agent?

2. Who/what is the host?

3. Who/what is the environment (reservoir/mode of transmission)?

4. In the past year, there have been 10 deaths of infants under 1 year of age and 300 live births in a community. What is the infant mortality rate for this community?

Chapter 3: Epidemiological Perspective

Application Exercises Answer Key

Scenario: A client presents with measles.

1. Who/what is the agent?

   The rubeola virus is the agent. Agents are biological, chemical, or physical. They can be bacteria, viruses, fungi, pesticides, food additives, or radiation.

2. Who/what is the host?

   The client who is infected is the host. The host is a living organism capable of being infected or affected by the agent under natural conditions.

3. Who/what is the environment (reservoir/mode of transmission)?

   In this situation, the environment is the human reservoir. The environment is all that is external to the host, including how the agent was transmitted.

4. In the past year, there have been 10 deaths of infants under 1 year of age and 300 live births in a community. What is the infant mortality rate for this community?

$$\frac{\text{\# of Deaths}}{\text{Population Total}} \times 1{,}000 = \underline{\hspace{2cm}} \text{ per } 1{,}000$$

$$\frac{10 \text{ Deaths}}{300 \text{ Live Births}} \times 1{,}000 = 33 \text{ per } 1{,}000 \text{ Births}$$

Chapter 4:	Ethical Decision Making and Client Rights in the Community

Contributor: Patricia Thompson, PhD, MSPH, RN

 Learning Objectives:

Δ   Describe how ethics is a key function of community health nurses.

Δ   Discuss client rights.

Δ   Discuss ethical decision-making processes.

Δ   Discuss advocacy and community health nursing.

 Key Points

Δ   The Public Health Code of Ethics identifies the ethical practice of public health. Ethical considerations include preventing harm, doing no harm, promoting good, respecting both individual and community rights, respecting autonomy and diversity, and providing confidentiality, competency, trustworthiness, and advocacy.

Δ   Community health nurses are concerned with protecting, promoting, preserving, and maintaining health, as well as preventing disease. These concerns reflect the ethical principle of promoting good and preventing harm. Balancing individual rights versus rights of community groups is a challenge.

Δ   Community health nurses address the challenges of autonomy and providing ethical care.

Δ   Client rights include the right to information disclosure, privacy, informed consent, information confidentiality, and participation in treatment decisions.

Application of Ethical Principles to Community Health Nursing		
Ethical Principles	**Definition**	**Community Health Nursing Situations**
Respect for Autonomy	Individuals select those actions that fulfill their goals.	Client right to self-determination (e.g., making a decision not to pursue chemotherapy)
Nonmaleficence	No harm is done when applying standards of care.	Developing plans of care that include a system for monitoring and evaluating outcomes
Beneficence	Maximize possible benefits and minimize possible harms.	Assessment of risk and benefits
Distributive Justice	Fair distribution of the benefits and burden in society is based on the needs and contributions of its members.	Determining who will be eligible for health care services based on income and fiscal resources

Ethical Decision Making

Δ There are several theories for ethical decision making. Generally, each includes:

- Assessing the situation.

- Determining the ethical issues associated with the problem (autonomy, beneficence, nonmaleficence, justice).

- Developing options.

- Involving individuals who should make decisions.

- Deciding on an option to implement.

- Implementing the option with consideration to the nursing code of ethics, all federal and state laws affecting the actions, and the values of all involved.

- Evaluating the outcome of the actions.

Δ Ethics committees are interdisciplinary teams that assist in ethical decision making. The underlying goals of ethics committees are to promote:

- The rights of clients.

- Shared decision making between clients (or their designees) and their health care providers.

- Fair policies and procedures that increase the likelihood of reaching client-centered outcomes.

Advocacy

Δ   Advocacy is the act of supporting clients' rights by respecting their decisions and enhancing their autonomy.

Δ   The intrinsic values to basic client advocacy are:

- The client is an autonomous being who has the right to make decisions affecting his own health and welfare.

- The client has the right to expect a nurse-client relationship that is based on shared respect, trust, collaboration related to health, and consideration of the client's thoughts and feelings.

- The client is responsible for his own health.

- It is the nurse's responsibility to ensure access to services that meet the client's health care needs.

Δ   Duties within the advocate role include:

- Informer: Inform the client about her rights and any information that will assist her in decision making without bias.

- Supporter: Support the decisions of the client while remaining objective and respecting the cultural, religious, or other influences the client uses in making those decisions. Support and respect the inherent right of each client to make her own decisions regardless of personal agreement with those decisions.

- Mediator: Act as a mediator on the client's behalf. Intervene when the client is experiencing conflict and requires assistance to solve a problem.

Δ   The community health nurse assesses and knows the needs of the client and specific populations and the resources within communities. The nurse uses that knowledge to affect the quality of care as a client advocate.

Δ   As an advocate, the nurse can influence health policies at the institutional, local, state, and federal levels.

Δ   Advocacy and ethical guidelines:

- Focus on the best interests of the client, group, and community.

- Carry out actions that are in agreement with the client, group, and community.

- Maintain communication with the client, group, and community.

- Implement actions.

- Provide independent opinions.

- Respect confidentiality.

Primary Reference:

Stanhope, M., & Lancaster, J. (2006). *Foundations of nursing in the community: Community-oriented practice* (2nd ed.). St. Louis, MO: Mosby.

Chapter 4: Ethical Decision Making and Client Rights in the Community

Application Exercises

1. The principle of autonomy includes which of the following? (Select all that apply.)

_____ Protection of privacy

_____ Respect for person

_____ Egalitarian approach

_____ Informed consent

_____ Fulfillment of client goals

Scenario: A community health nurse is providing care in the home to a 40-year-old client who has been diagnosed with amyotrophic lateral sclerosis (ALS). The client is married and has three children, ages 5, 8, and 11. He had been employed as a life insurance agent most of his adult life but had to quit his job during the past 6 months due to progression of the disease. His wife has also had to take a leave of absence from her job to help care for her husband at home. The family is experiencing multiple financial strains due to the sudden loss of incomes. The client's disease is continuing to progress; soon, the client and his family will need to decide if he should receive mechanical ventilation. The client asks the nurse to help him decide what he should do.

---

2. What factors should the nurse consider when helping a client make a decision in this situation?

3. What nursing interventions should the nurse use when helping the client come to a decision?

4. What role would an ethics committee play in this situation?

5. How does the principle of autonomy apply to this situation?

Chapter 4: Ethical Decision Making and Client Rights in the Community

Application Exercises Answer Key

1. The principle of autonomy includes which of the following? (Select all that apply.)

   __X__ **Protection of privacy**
   __X__ **Respect for person**
   _____ Egalitarian approach
   __X__ **Informed consent**
   __X__ **Fulfillment of client goals**

   Autonomy is the capacity to be one's own person and to live one's life according to self-determined reasons and motives that are not the product of external forces. Recognizing a client's autonomy displays respect for person, protects client rights (including the right to privacy), ensures informed consent, and allows for the fulfillment of client goals.

Scenario: A community health nurse is providing care in the home to a 40-year-old client who has been diagnosed with amyotrophic lateral sclerosis (ALS). The client is married and has three children, ages 5, 8, and 11. He had been employed as a life insurance agent most of his adult life but had to quit his job during the past 6 months due to progression of the disease. His wife has also had to take a leave of absence from her job to help care for her husband at home. The family is experiencing multiple financial strains due to the sudden loss of incomes. The client's disease is continuing to progress; soon, the client and his family will need to decide if he should receive mechanical ventilation. The client asks the nurse to help him decide what he should do.

---

2. What factors should the nurse consider when helping a client make a decision in this situation?

   Client and family's past experiences
   Client and family's outlook for the future
   Client's fears
   Client and family's ability to cope with disease
   Client and family's religious beliefs
   Anything that has impacted the client and family in the past, present, and future

3. What nursing interventions should the nurse use when helping the client come to a decision?

Allow the client and family to make their own choice.
Help guide the client and family to work through their emotions and the decision-making process.
Be aware of personal thoughts and feelings regarding this issue so as not to impose them onto the client and family.
Maintain a professional relationship with the client and family.

4. What role would an ethics committee play in this situation?

An ethics committee could help in the decision-making process and give recommendations. An ethics committee is an interdisciplinary team that assists in decisions with ethical issues, client values, and professional obligations.

5. How does the principle of autonomy apply to this situation?

The principle of autonomy applies to the client's decision about receiving mechanical ventilation. It is the client and family's decision. Even if the nurse feels strongly about not using a ventilator to sustain life, she should not try to convince the family to see things the same way. Autonomy is having independence and freedom from control by external forces. Health care providers should promote independence, ensure the client's right to privacy, protect the client's right to confidentiality, and ensure informed consent prior to the client's participation in a procedure, treatment, or research.

Chapter 5:   Cultural Awareness

Contributor: Patricia Thompson, PhD, MSPH, RN

 Learning Objectives:

Δ   Discuss culture and the importance of congruency between culture and health care.

Δ   Discuss the importance of the community health nurse's development of cultural awareness and cultural competence.

Δ   Identify some of the components of a cultural assessment.

Δ   Identify culturally sensitive interventions.

 Key Points

Δ   Culture is defined as a set of beliefs, values, and assumptions about life that are widely held among a group of people and that are transmitted across generations.

Δ   Acculturation is the process of learning a new culture. Adapting to a new culture requires changes in daily living practices. These changes relate to language, education, work, recreation, social experiences, and the health care system.

Δ   Congruency between culture and health care is essential to the well-being of the client. The link between health beliefs and practices is culture.

Δ   It is important to assess cultural beliefs and practices when determining a plan of care. The community health nurse needs to consider that not all cultures are similar, and there are variations within each culture. The uniqueness of each client needs to be considered.

Δ   Cultural awareness includes self-awareness of one's own cultural background, biases, and differences. Health care professionals need to assess their own beliefs and ask themselves how those beliefs may affect the care given to clients.

Δ   Cultural competence is knowing, appreciating, and considering the culture of someone else in resolving problems.

Δ   A cultural assessment provides information to the health care providers about the effect of culture on communication, space and physical contact, time, social organization, biologic variation, and environmental control factors.

General Cultural-Assessment Parameters

- Δ Ethnic background

- Δ Religious preferences

- Δ Family structure

- Δ Language

- Δ Communication needs

- Δ Education

- Δ Cultural values

- Δ Food patterns

- Δ Health practices

The Three Steps of Data Collection

- Δ Collection of self-identifying data

- Δ Posing questions that address the client's perceptions of his health needs

- Δ Identification of cultural factors that may impact the choice of nursing interventions

Using an Interpreter

- Δ An interpreter should be used when it is difficult for the nurse or client to understand the other's language. It is recommended to select an interpreter who has knowledge of health-related terminology. The use of family members as interpreters is generally not advisable, since clients may need privacy in discussing sensitive matters. Health teaching materials should be available in the client's primary language.

Cultural Competence: Areas for Self-Assessment

- Δ Am I aware of my culture and views I have about other cultures?

- Δ Am I able to do a culturally sensitive assessment?

- Δ Do I have the knowledge necessary to develop nursing interventions?

- Δ What is my experience in working with diverse populations?

- Δ What is my goal in learning about diverse populations?

Conveying Cultural Sensitivity

Δ The nurse should address clients by their last names, unless the client gives the nurse permission to use other names.

Δ The nurse should introduce himself by name and explain his position.

Δ The nurse should be authentic and honest about what he does or does not know about a client's culture.

Δ Use language that is culturally sensitive.

Δ Find out what clients know about their health problems and treatments, and assess cultural congruence.

Δ Do not make assumptions about clients.

Δ Encourage clients to ask about anything that they may not understand.

Δ Respect clients' values, beliefs, and practices.

Δ Show respect for clients' support systems.

Primary Reference:

Stanhope, M., & Lancaster, J. (2006). *Foundations of nursing in the community: Community-oriented practice* (2nd ed.). St. Louis, MO: Mosby.

Additional Resources:

Leininger, M., & McFarland, M. R. (2002). *Transcultural nursing: Concepts, theories, research & practice* (3rd ed.). New York: McGraw-Hill.

Chapter 5: Cultural Awareness

Application Exercises

1. Culture can be defined as

    A. a set of beliefs, values, and assumptions about life.

    B. ethnocentric patterns of life.

    C. a changed belief system.

    D. explicit behaviors and beliefs.

2. A male client from Japan does not make eye contact with a nurse when she speaks. This nonverbal behavior is indicative of which of the following?

    A. The client has low self-esteem.

    B. The client is exhibiting signs of fatigue.

    C. The client has a negative attitude toward the nurse.

    D. Further assessment is needed of the client's culture and his feelings before a determination can be made.

3. A family from Somalia moves to the United States. They move to a Somalian neighborhood, learn to speak English, and acknowledge Somalian and U.S. holidays. This process is known as

    A. modification.

    B. enculturation.

    C. acculturation.

    D. adjusting.

4. An older adult woman from Croatia has been diagnosed with grade 4 breast cancer. She agrees that her family should be told that she has cancer, but she feels that information regarding the severity of her diagnosis should be withheld. Which of the following reflects a culturally sensitive nursing intervention?

    A. Contact an ethics committee to resolve the situation.

    B. Arrange for hospice care.

    C. Discuss the need for the client to get her "affairs" together.

    D. Establish a meeting with the client, family, and health team to discuss the client's diagnosis per the client's guidelines.

Chapter 5: Cultural Awareness

Application Exercises Answer Key

1. Culture can be defined as

   A. a set of beliefs, values, and assumptions about life.

   B. ethnocentric patterns of life.

   C. a changed belief system.

   D. explicit behaviors and beliefs.

   Culture is defined as a set of beliefs, values, and assumptions about life that are widely held among a group of people and that are transmitted across generations.

2. A male client from Japan does not make eye contact with a nurse when she speaks. This nonverbal behavior is indicative of which of the following?

   A. The client has low self-esteem.

   B. The client is exhibiting signs of fatigue.

   C. The client has a negative attitude toward the nurse.

   D. Further assessment is needed of the client's culture and his feelings before a determination can be made.

   It is important to avoid assumptions about the client's feelings and culture. Further assessment will provide greater insight into how to interpret his avoidance of eye contact.

3. A family from Somalia moves to the United States. They move to a Somalian neighborhood, learn to speak English, and acknowledge Somalian and U.S. holidays. This process is known as

   A. modification.

   B. enculturation.

   C. acculturation.

   D. adjusting.

   Acculturation is the process of learning a new culture. Adapting to a new culture will require changes in daily living practices. These changes frequently relate to language, education, work, recreation, social experiences, and the health care system.

4. An older adult woman from Croatia has been diagnosed with grade 4 breast cancer. She agrees that her family should be told that she has cancer, but she feels that information regarding the severity of her diagnosis should be withheld. Which of the following reflects a culturally sensitive nursing intervention?

    A. Contact an ethics committee to resolve the situation.

    B. Arrange for hospice care.

    C. Discuss the need for the client to get her "affairs" together.

    D. Establish a meeting with the client, family, and health team to discuss the client's diagnosis per the client's guidelines.

It is important to respect the client's values, beliefs, and practices.

Chapter 6:   Community Health Education

Contributor: Carel Mountain, MSN, RN

 Learning Objectives:

△ Discuss the role of community health nurses in community health education.

△ Recognize educational issues relevant to planning and implementing a community health education plan, including barriers to learning.

△ Design a community health education plan based on an identified population-specific learning need.

△ Differentiate among learning styles and select instructional strategies based on learning style assessment findings.

 Key Points

△ Community health nurses regularly provide health education in order to promote, maintain, and restore the health of populations.

△ In designing community education programs, nurses must take into account the barriers that make learning difficult. Some of these obstacles include age, culture, poor reading and comprehension skills, language barriers, and lack of motivation.

△ Effective community health education requires planning.

Learning Theories

△ Behavioral theory: Focus is on changing behavior through the use of reinforcement methods.

△ Cognitive theory: Focus is on changing thought patterns through the use of methods that offer a variety of sensory input and repetition.

△ Critical theory: Focus is on increasing depth of knowledge through the use of methods such as discussion and inquiry.

△ Developmental theory: Focus is on the human developmental stage and methods that are age-specific and age-appropriate with importance given to "readiness to learn."

Δ   Humanistic theory: Focus is on feelings and relationships, and methods are based on the principle that learners will do what is in their best interests.

Δ   Social learning theory: Focus is on changing the learners' expectations and beliefs through the use of methods that link information to beliefs and values.

Learning Styles

Δ   Visual learners learn through "seeing" and methods such as note taking, video viewing, and presentations. These learners "think in pictures."

Δ   Auditory learners learn through "listening" and methods such as verbal lectures, discussion, and reading aloud. These learners "interpret meaning while listening."

Δ   Tactile-kinesthetic learners learn through "doing" and methods such as trial and error, hands-on approaches, and return demonstration. These learners gain "meaning through exploration."

Development of a Community Health Education Plan

Δ   Identify population-specific learning needs. Set priorities. Select the priority learning need.

Δ   Select aspects of learning theories (behavioral, cognitive, critical, developmental, humanistic, social learning) to use in the educational program based on the identified learning need.

Δ   Consider educational issues such as population-specific concerns, barriers to learning, and learning styles (visual, auditory, tactile-kinesthetic).

Δ   Design the educational program.

- Set short- and long-term learning objectives that are measurable and achievable.

- Select an appropriate educational method based on learning objectives and assessment of participants' learning styles.

- Select content appropriate to learning objectives and allotted time frame.

- Select an evaluation method that will provide feedback regarding achievement of short-term learning objectives.

Δ   Implement the education program. Ensure an environment that is conducive to learning (minimal distractions; favorable to interaction, learner comfort, and readability).

Δ   Evaluate the achievement of learning objectives and the effectiveness of instruction.

Primary Reference:

Stanhope, M., & Lancaster, J. (2006). *Foundations of nursing in the community: Community-oriented practice* (2nd ed.). St. Louis, MO: Mosby.

Chapter 6: Community Health Education

Application Exercises

Scenario: A community health nurse identifies the need for a community health education program regarding breast self-examination for a population of older adult women at a wellness center within the community. Most of the women are Spanish speaking. The nurse decides to show a short video about breast self-examination followed by a discussion of the technique for breast self-examination. The nurse will also have a mannequin available for participants to use to practice breast self-examination techniques.

1. What are potential educational issues to be considered specific to this population?

2. Write appropriate short- and long-term learning objectives for this educational program.

3. This program is designed to educate what types of learners?

4. Six months after the initiation of the breast self-examination program for these women, how should the effectiveness of this program be measured?

Chapter 6: Community Health Education

Application Exercises Answer Key

Scenario: A community health nurse identifies the need for a community health education program regarding breast self-examination for a population of older adult women at a wellness center within the community. Most of the women are Spanish speaking. The nurse decides to show a short video about breast self-examination followed by a discussion of the technique for breast self-examination. The nurse will also have a mannequin available for participants to use to practice breast self-examination techniques.

1. What are potential educational issues to be considered specific to this population?

In designing community education programs, nurses must take into account the barriers that make learning difficult. Some of these obstacles include age, culture, poor reading and comprehension skills, language barriers, and lack of motivation. The age of this population may pose some issues, such as perceptions of minimal benefits of early detection and possibly some sensory-perceptual alterations. Use of an interpreter and a video in Spanish may need to be considered.

2. Write appropriate short- and long-term learning objectives for this educational program.

Short-term learning objective: Learners will be able to demonstrate appropriate breast self-examination techniques using the provided mannequin.

Long-term learning objective: Learners will routinely perform breast self-examinations.

3. This program is designed to educate what types of learners?

This program meets the needs of visual learners through the use of the video regarding breast self-examination, auditory learners through the use of discussion of the technique for performing breast self-examination, and tactile-kinesthetic learners through the hands-on approach of practicing breast self-examination techniques on the mannequin.

4. Six months after the initiation of the breast self-examination program for these women, how should the effectiveness of this program be measured?

Survey the participants regarding their performance of breast self-examinations, detection of lumps on breast self-examination, and whether or not they have educated others about breast self-examination.

Chapter 7:   Community Assessment and Diagnosis

Contributor: Patricia Thompson, PhD, MSPH, RN

 Learning Objectives:

Δ   Discuss the role of community assessments in the identification of community needs and problems, strengths, and resources.

Δ   Recognize data to be collected by community assessments.

Δ   Discuss appropriate methods for data collection.

Δ   Interpret data and establish priorities among identified problems.

 Key Points

Δ   Community assessment is a comprehensive approach that identifies the community as a client.

Δ   Community assessment and diagnosis are the foundation for population-specific program planning.

Δ   The community health nurse is a key player in assessing the needs of the community. This role includes:

•   Interacting with community partners serving the community at large.

•   Witnessing the interaction between community programs and the response of the client to the services.

•   Identifying future services based on the visible needs of population groups.

Components of a Community Assessment

Δ   People

•   Demographic: distribution, mobility, density, census data

•   Biological factors: health and disease status, genetics, race, age, gender, causes of death

•   Social factors: occupation, activities, marital status, education, income

•   Cultural factors: positions, roles, history, values, customs, norms, religion

Δ   Place or environment

- Physical factors: geography, terrain, type of community, location of health services

- Environmental factors: climate, flora, fauna, topography, toxic substances, vectors, pollutants

Δ   Social systems

- Health systems

- Economic systems/factors

- Education systems

- Religious systems

- Welfare systems

- Political systems

- Recreation systems/factors

- Legal systems

- Communication systems/factors

- Transportation systems

- Resources and services

Data Collection

Δ   Data collection is a critical community health nursing function.

Data Collection Method	Description	Strengths	Limitations
Informant interviews	Direct discussion with community members for the purpose of obtaining ideas and opinions from key informants	• Minimal cost • Participants serving as future supporters	• Built in bias • Meeting time and place
Community forum	Open public meeting	• Opportunity for community input • Minimal cost	• Difficulty finding a convenient time and place • Potential to drift from the issue • Possibility that a less vocal person may be reluctant to speak

Data Collection Method	Description	Strengths	Limitations
Compiling data from various sources	Use of existing (secondary) data (e.g., death statistics, birth statistics, census data, mortality and morbidity data) to assess problem	• Database of prior concerns/needs of population	• Possibility that data may not represent current situation
Windshield survey	Descriptive approach that assesses several community components by driving through a community	• Provides a descriptive overview of a community	• Need for a driver so the nurse can attend to note-taking about the community elements • May be time consuming
Focus groups	Directed talk with a representative sample	• Minimal cost • Possibility of participants being potential supporters • Provides insight into community support	• Time consuming • Possible discussion of irrelevant issues
Surveys	Specific questions asked in a written format	• Data collected on client population and problems • Random sampling	• Low response rate • Expensive • Time consuming • Possibility of the collection of superficial data
Participant observation	Observation of formal or informal community activities	• Indication of community priorities and environmental profile • Identification of power structures	• Bias

Δ   Windshield Survey Components

- People

  ◊   Who is on the street?

  ◊   How are they dressed?

  ◊   What are they doing?

  ◊   What is the origin, ethnicity, or race of the people?

  ◊   How are the different groups (subgroups) residentially located?

  ◊   How should the nurse categorize the socioeconomic status of the residents? Why?

  ◊   Is there any evidence of drug abuse, violence, disease, mental illness? If yes, why does the nurse think so?

  ◊   Are there any animals or pets in the community?

- Place

  ◊   Boundaries

    °   Where is the community located?

    °   What are its boundaries?

    °   Are there natural boundaries?

    °   Are there human-made boundaries?

  ◊   Location of health services

    °   Where are the major health facilities located?

    °   What health care facilities are necessary for the community but are not within the community?

  ◊   Natural environment

    °   Are there geographic features that may harm the community?

    °   Are there plants or animals that could harm or threaten the health of the community?

  ◊   Human-made environment

    °   What industries are within the community?

    °   Could these pose a threat to the health of community workers or the community itself?

    °   Is there easy access to health care facilities?

    °   Are the roads adequate and marked well?

◊   Housing

    °   Is the housing of acceptable quality?

    °   How old are the homes?

    °   Are there single or multifamily dwellings?

    °   Is the housing in good repair or disrepair?

    °   Is there vacant housing? Why?

◊   Social systems

    °   Are there social services, clinics, hospitals, dentists, clinics, and health care providers available within the community?

    °   Are there ample schools within the community? Are they in good repair or disrepair?

    °   Are there parks or areas for recreation?

    °   What places of worship are within the community?

    °   What services are provided by local religious groups, schools, community centers, and activity or recreation centers?

    °   Is there public transportation? Is it effective?

    °   What grocery stores or other stores are within the community?

    °   Is public protection evident (e.g., police, fire, EMS services)?

Analysis of Community Assessment Data

Δ   The community health nurse plays an active role in assessment, data interpretation, and problem identification. Steps in analysis of community assessment data include:

- Gather collected data into a composite database.

- Assess completeness of data.

- Identify and generate missing data.

- Synthesize data and identify themes.

- Identify community needs and problems.

- Identify community strengths and resources.

Δ   Problem analysis is completed for each identified problem. Frequently, work groups are formed to examine individual problems and develop solutions.

Δ   In the problem statement, the nurse should identify expected outcomes based on specific and measurable criteria.

Community Health Diagnoses

Δ   Problems identified by community assessments are often stated as community health diagnoses.

Δ   Community nursing diagnoses incorporate information from the community assessment, general nursing knowledge, and epidemiological concepts (especially the concept of risk in a population).

Δ   Community nursing diagnoses often are written in the following format:

- Risk of (specific problem or risk in the community) among (the specific population that is affected by the problem or risk) related to (strengths and weaknesses in the community that influence the problem or risk).

Establishing Priorities Among Identified Problems

Δ   In setting priorities among identified community problems, factors to be considered include:

- Community awareness of the problem.

- Community readiness to tackle the problem.

- Available expertise/fiscal resources.

- Severity of the problem.

- Amount of time needed for problem resolution.

Primary Reference:

Stanhope, M., & Lancaster, J. (2006). *Foundations of nursing in the community: Community-oriented practice* (2nd ed.). St. Louis, MO: Mosby.

Chapter 7: Community Assessment and Diagnosis

Application Exercises

1. Directed conversation with select members of a community about a health problem is the data assessment method known as

    A. key informant interviews.

    B. participant observation.

    C. focus groups.

    D. windshield survey.

2. Which of the following are examples of sources for secondary data? (Select all that apply.)

    _____ Birth statistics

    _____ Death statistics

    _____ Previous health survey results

    _____ Minutes from past community meetings

    _____ Windshield survey

    _____ Community forum

    _____ Health records

Scenario: A community health nurse collects data for a community assessment. The following information is noted about the community:

    Low crime rate
    Weekly curbside garbage pick-up
    Small amount of litter along the road
    Public transportation that operates 24 hr a day, 7 days a week
    Many opportunities for residents to be active in the community, including several community organizations
    Recreational trails that are in need of maintenance and repair

---

3. What methods were most likely used to collect these data?

4. What is an appropriate community health diagnosis for this community?

Chapter 7: Community Assessment and Diagnosis

Application Exercises Answer Key

1. Directed conversation with select members of a community about a health problem is the data assessment method known as

A. key informant interviews.
B. participant observation.
C. focus groups.
D. windshield survey.

Informant interviews are direct discussions with community members for the purpose of obtaining ideas and opinions. Participant observation is the observation of formal or informal community activities. Focus groups are directed talk with a representative sample. Windshield survey is a descriptive approach that assesses several community components by driving through a community.

2. Which of the following are examples of sources for secondary data? (Select all that apply.)

  X   **Birth statistics**
  X   **Death statistics**
  X   **Previous health survey results**
  X   **Minutes from past community meetings**
       Windshield survey
       Community forum
  X   **Health records**

Birth statistics, death statistics, previous health survey results, minutes from past community meetings, and health records are all sources for secondary data. Windshield survey and community forum are data collection methods.

Scenario: A community health nurse collects data for a community assessment. The following information is noted about the community:

Low crime rate
Weekly curbside garbage pick-up
Small amount of litter along the road
Public transportation that operates 24 hr a day, 7 days a week
Many opportunities for residents to be active in the community, including several community organizations
Recreational trails that are in need of maintenance and repair

3. What methods were most likely used to collect these data?

Likely methods include (but are not limited to):

Low crime rate: Obtaining statistics at city hall (secondary data)
Weekly curbside garbage pick-up: Interviewing the city mayor (informant interview)
Small amount of litter along the road: Driving through the community (windshield survey)
Public transportation that operates 24 hr a day, 7 days a week: Interviewing the city mayor (informant interview)
Many opportunities for residents to be active in the community, including several community organizations: Interviewing a parent-teacher association (focus group)
Recreational trails that are in need of maintenance and repair: Driving through the community (windshield survey)

4. What is an appropriate community health diagnosis for this community?

Risk of injury among children related to recreational trails that are in need of maintenance and repair

Chapter 8:	**Community Health Program Planning and Evaluation**
	Contributor: Patricia Thompson, PhD, MSPH, RN

 Learning Objectives:

Δ   Discuss the role of the community health nurse in community health program planning.

Δ   Discuss the phases involved in community health program planning and the role of the community health nurse in each phase.

Δ   Discuss strategies and barriers for implementation of community health programs.

Δ   Discuss appropriate methods for evaluation of the effectiveness of community health programs and initiatives.

 Key Points

Δ   The role of the community health nurse in community health program planning and evaluation is a **collaborative leadership role**. The desired outcome is to plan, organize, implement, and evaluate intervention programs that address the health needs of the community.

Δ   Community health program planning should reflect the priorities set as a result of analysis of community assessment data. Priorities are established based on the extent of the problem (e.g., percent of population affected by the problem), the relevance of the problem to the public (e.g., degree of risk, economic loss), and the estimated impact of intervention (e.g., improvement of health outcome, adverse effects).

Community Health Program Planning

Planning Phases	Description	Activities	Community Health Nursing Role
Preplanning	Brainstorm ideas.	Obtain community awareness, support, and involvement.	• Collaborate in developing a problem statement, goal statement, and timeline. • Assess resources and develop interventions with community partners.
Assessment	Collect data about the population.	Evaluate the trends and risk factors of the population for the identified health need.	• Complete a needs assessment and identify community strengths. • Develop priorities and establish outcomes.
Policy development	Plan interventions to meet identified outcomes, focusing on education, enforcement, and engineering elements.	Establish methods for allocating the resources and ascertaining rights, status, and resources.	• Initiate interventions to meet outcomes by linking resources to needs, developing community partnerships, and planning interventions that impact health protection and promotion and disease prevention.
Implementation	Carry out the plan.	Identify the sequence of interventions and when they should occur.	• Monitor the intervention process and the response of the community in terms of its values, needs, and perceptions.
Evaluation	Examine the success of the interventions.	Document the progress of the interventions, compare the outcomes against a standard, and modify the interventions based on results.	• Conduct formative and summative evaluations. • Modify the interventions to meet the needs of the population. • Share findings with population groups.

Development of a Plan for a Community Health Program

Δ   Establish goals and objectives. Generally, the goal is to decrease the incidence and prevalence of the identified problem. Objectives are behaviorally stated, measurable, and include a target date for achievement.

Δ   Select strategies/interventions to meet the objectives.

Δ   Plan a logical sequence for interventions by establishing a timetable.

Δ   Identify who will assume responsibility for each intervention.

Δ   Assess the personnel needed and any special training they may require for screening or providing education.

Δ   Assess supplies, equipment, educational materials, office space, locations for screenings, and educational services.

Δ   Develop a budget.

Δ   Plan for program evaluation.

Δ   Implement the program.

Δ   Evaluate the program.

Strategies and Barriers in Implementing Community Health Programs

Helpful Strategies	Barriers
Thorough assessment	Inadequate assessment
Accurate interpretation of data	Inadequate or misconstrued data
Collaboration with community partners	No involvement with community partners
Effective communication patterns	Impaired communication
Sufficient resources	Inadequate resources
Logical planning	Lack of planning
Skilled leadership	Poor leadership

Community Health Program Evaluation

Δ   It is important to remember that evaluation is an ongoing process.

Δ   Program evaluation should document not only success in meeting outcomes but also the efficiency and effectiveness of the program plan and specific interventions.

Δ   Evaluation is needed throughout the program to respond to the changing needs of the population.

Primary Reference:

Stanhope, M., & Lancaster, J. (2006). *Foundations of nursing in the community: Community-oriented practice* (2nd ed.). St. Louis, MO: Mosby.

Chapter 8: Community Health Program Planning and Evaluation

Application Exercises

1. Identify strategies for successful implementation of health programs.

2. Identify barriers for successful implementation of health programs.

3. A community health nurse is evaluating a community health program designed to promote car safety for infants. The program was implemented 2 years ago. Explain how the nurse should identify appropriate program evaluation steps.

Chapter 8: Community Health Program Planning and Evaluation

Application Exercises Answer Key

1. Identify strategies for successful implementation of health programs.

   Accurate assessment of need, active involvement of community participants in identifying the health problem, adequate resources, logical planning, community partnerships, and leadership

2. Identify barriers for successful implementation of health programs.

   Poor assessment, disagreement of what the health problem is, lack of leadership, lack of resources, insufficient community involvement, and poor planning

3. A community health nurse is evaluating a community health program designed to promote car safety for infants. The program was implemented 2 years ago. Explain how the nurse should identify appropriate program evaluation steps.

   Determine if the program goals and objectives were met. Pose questions (e.g., "How many parents attended the educational program about infant car seat safety?"). Identify the number of correctly installed car seats. Compare/contrast rates of prior car seat use with current rates of car seat use and investigate if there has been a decline in infant injury or death related to changes in the use of car seats.

   Gather feedback by asking parents questions (e.g., "What was helpful about the car safety program?", "What areas should be improved?", "Overall, were you satisfied with the program?", "Might you recommend the program to other parents?").

Chapter 9:	Community Health Resources
	Contributor: Patricia Thompson, PhD, MSPH, RN

 Learning Objectives:

Δ   Describe the role and responsibilities of community health nurses in making referrals.

Δ   Discuss barriers to health care access and the role of community health nurses in assessing and ensuring accessibility of health care services.

Δ   Discuss the roles of international, federal, state, and local health organizations in the promotion of the health of populations.

Δ   Discuss financing options for the provision of community health resources.

Referrals

Δ   The community health nurse plays a significant role in the referral process.

Δ   Nurses link clients to community resources.

Δ   The nurse educates clients about community resources and self-care measures.

Δ   Steps in the referral process include:

- Engaging in a working relationship with the client.

- Establishing criteria for the referral.

- Exploring resources.

- Accepting the client's decision to use a given resource.

- Making the referral.

- Facilitating the referral.

- Evaluating the outcome.

Δ   Barriers to the Referral Process

Client Barriers	Resource Barriers
• Lack of motivation • Inadequate information about community resources • Inadequate understanding of the need for referral • Accessibility needs • Priorities • Finances • Cultural factors	• Attitudes of health care personnel • Costs of services • Physical accessibility of resources • Time limitations • Limited expertise working with culturally diverse populations

Δ   Follow-up considerations include:

•   Monitoring the client if the referral was completed.

•   Assessing whether referral outcomes were met.

•   Determining if the client was satisfied with the referral.

Access to Health Care

Δ   Community assessment includes evaluating the adequacy of health services within the community and their accessibility by those in need of services.

Δ   Barriers to health care include:

•   Inadequate health care insurance.

•   Inability to pay for health care services.

•   Language barriers.

•   Cultural barriers.

•   Lack of health care providers in a community.

•   Geographic isolation.

•   Social isolation.

•   Lack of communication tools (e.g., telephones).

•   Lack of personal or public transportation to health care facilities.

•   Inconvenient hours.

•   Attitudes of health care personnel toward clients of low socioeconomic status or those with different cultural/ethnic backgrounds.

•   Eligibility requirements for state/federal assistance programs.

Δ   Community health nurses are responsible for increasing the access to health care for vulnerable populations (e.g., children, older adults, clients who are physically/mentally disabled, unemployed, or homeless).

Δ   Community health nurses advocate for the accessibility of health care services.

Health Care Organizations and Financing

Δ   **International Health Organizations**

- World Health Organization (WHO)

  ◊   Provides daily information regarding the occurrence of internationally important diseases.

  ◊   Establishes world standards for antibiotics and vaccines.

  ◊   The WHO primarily focuses on the health care workforce and education, environment, sanitation, infectious diseases, maternal and child health, and primary care.

Δ   **Federal Health Agencies**

- U.S. Department of Health & Human Services

  ◊   Under the direction of the secretary of health.

  ◊   Funded through federal taxes.

  ◊   Consists of 12 agencies.

    °   Administration for Children and Families

    °   Administration on Aging

    °   Centers for Medicare and Medicaid Services – also administers the Health Insurance Portability and Accountability Act (HIPAA), disability insurance, Aid to Families with Dependent Children (AFDC), and Supplemental Security Income (SSI).

Medicare	Medicaid
• Medicare provides hospital and medical insurance to individuals who are 65 years and older, permanently disabled, and/or have end-stage renal failure. • Part A (hospital care, home care, limited skilled nursing care) • Part B (medical care, diagnostic services, physiotherapy)	• Medicaid provides financial assistance to states and counties to pay for health care services for older adults with low socioeconomic status, clients with disabilities, and families with dependent children. • Medicaid provides inpatient and outpatient hospital care, laboratory and radiology services, physician services, skilled nursing care at home or in a nursing home for persons older than 21 years, and early periodic screening, diagnosis, and treatment for those younger than 21 years.

- ° Agency for Healthcare Research and Quality
- ° Centers for Disease Control and Prevention – works to prevent and control disease, injury, and disability both nationally and internationally.
- ° Agency for Toxic Substances and Disease Registry
- ° Food and Drug Administration
- ° Health Resources and Service Administration – includes the Division of Nursing and the Divisions of Medicine, Dentistry, and Allied Health Professions.
- ° Indian Health Service
- ° National Institutes of Health – supports biomedical research and includes the National Institute of Nursing Research.
- ° Substance Abuse and Mental Health Services Administration
- ° Office of the Secretary
- • Veterans Health Administration (within the U.S. Department of Veterans Affairs) – finances health services for active and retired military persons and dependents.

Δ State Health Departments

- • State departments of public health nursing, which manage the Women, Infants, and Children (WIC) program, are part of state health departments.
- • State Children's Health Insurance Program (SCHIP) – offers expanded health care coverage to uninsured children.
- • Board of Examiners of Nurses
    - ◊ State Practice Act
    - ◊ Licensing and examination of registered and licensed practical nurses (in some states known as licensed vocational nurses)
    - ◊ Approval/oversight of schools of nursing
    - ◊ Revocation, suspension, or denial of nursing licenses
- • Establishment of public health codes
- • Assistance/support for local health departments
- • Funded through state taxes and federal funding
- • Administration of Medicaid programs
- • Nursing roles: advocate, teacher, coordinator, and consultant

Δ   **Local Health Department**

- The primary focus of a local health department is the health of its citizens.

- Local health departments offer various services and programs.

- The local community health nurse typically provides direct services such as referring caregivers of family members who are terminally ill to respite care and/or hospice services.

- Local health departments are funded through local taxes with support from federal and state funds.

- Nursing roles: advocate, teacher, coordinator, and consultant

Δ   **Private Funding**

- Health insurance

- Employer benefits

- Managed care

  ◊   Health maintenance organizations (HMOs) – Comprehensive care is provided to members by a set of designated providers.

  ◊   Preferred provider organizations (PPOs) – Predetermined rates are set for services delivered to members; financial incentives are in place to promote use of PPO providers.

  ◊   Medical savings accounts – Untaxed money is put in an account for use for medical expenses.

Primary Reference:

Stanhope, M., & Lancaster, J. (2006). *Foundations of nursing in the community: Community-oriented practice* (2nd ed.). St. Louis, MO: Mosby.

Additional Resources:

For more information about federal health care agencies, go to the U.S. Department of Health & Human Services Web site, *www.hhs.gov*.

Chapter 9: Community Health Resources

Application Exercises

1. Which of the following are responsibilities of local health departments? (Select all that apply.)

_____ Drug approval and control

_____ Assessment of the health status of populations

_____ Coordination of directives from state and federal levels

_____ Determination of how well community health needs are being met

_____ Licensing of registered nurses

2. The Division of Nursing is included within which of the following agencies?

A. National Center for Nursing Research

B. National Institute of Health

C. Bureau of Health Professions

D. Health Resources and Service Administration

3. The National Institute of Nursing Research is a section of which of the following?

A. Food and Drug Administration

B. National Institutes of Health

C. Bureau of Health Personnel Development and Service

D. Health Resources and Service Administration

4. A community health nurse is speaking with a 64-year-old client who recently moved to the state and has no health insurance. The client is a veteran and lives on a limited income. What can the nurse tell him about his options for health insurance?

5. A community health nurse is speaking with a young adult mother of two children who has just lost her job. She previously had health insurance through her employer. What can the nurse tell her about options for health insurance?

Chapter 9: Community Health Resources

Application Exercises Answer Key

1. Which of the following are responsibilities of local health departments? (Select all that apply.)

_____ Drug approval and control

__X__ **Assessment of the health status of populations**

__X__ **Coordination of directives from state and federal levels**

__X__ **Determination of how well community health needs are being met**

_____ Licensing of registered nurses

Local health departments are responsible for assessment of the health status of populations within their community and determining if the health needs of the community are being met. Local health departments are funded by federal and state taxes and therefore must coordinate directives from those levels. Approval and control of drugs is the responsibility of the Food and Drug Administration, which is a federal health agency. Licensing of registered nurses takes place at the state level.

2. The Division of Nursing is included within which of the following agencies?

A. National Center for Nursing Research

B. National Institute of Health

C. Bureau of Health Professions

D. Health Resources and Service Administration

The Health Resources and Service Administration includes the Division of Nursing and the Divisions of Medicine, Dentistry, and Allied Health Professions.

3. The National Institute of Nursing Research is a section of which of the following?

A. Food and Drug Administration

B. National Institutes of Health

C. Bureau of Health Personnel Development and Service

D. Health Resources and Service Administration

The National Institutes of Health supports biomedical research and includes the National Institute of Nursing Research (NINR).

4. A community health nurse is speaking with a 64-year-old client who recently moved to the state and has no health insurance. The client is a veteran and lives on a limited income. What can the nurse tell him about his options for health insurance?

Because the client is a veteran, he could receive health care services through the Veterans Health Administration. He may also be eligible for Medicaid services, which are provided by each state. When the client turns 65, he will be eligible for Medicare, which is a national health insurance plan for older adults.

5. A community health nurse is speaking with a young adult mother of two children who has just lost her job. She previously had health insurance through her employer. What can the nurse tell her about options for health insurance?

The Child Health Insurance Program (CHIP) provides expanded Medicaid coverage to children. They may also qualify for Medicaid benefits depending on the eligibility requirements of their state. The nurse should also make the client aware of the Health Insurance Portability and Accountability Act (HIPAA) of 1996, which is intended to provide health insurance coverage to people who lose their jobs.

Chapter 10:   Roles and Settings in Community Health Nursing

Contributors: Vera C. Brancato, EdD, MSN, RN-BC
Janet T. Ihlenfeld, PhD, RN
Carel Mountain, MSN, RN

 Learning Objectives:

Δ   Compare and contrast the roles and functions of home health, hospice, occupational health, school, and parish nurses and case managers.

Δ   Identify the primary focus of home health, hospice, occupational health, school, and parish nursing and case management.

Home Health Nurses

Δ   Home health nursing is a means for providing health care services to clients where they reside. This includes traditional homes, mobile homes, apartments, assisted living facilities, and nursing homes.

Δ   Nurses, physical therapists, occupational therapists, home health aides, social workers, and dietitians may be part of the interdisciplinary care provided in the home. These services are prescribed by a primary care provider and overseen by a nurse or physical therapist.

Δ   The home health nurse functions as educator, provider of skilled nursing interventions, and coordinator of care. Many clients leave the hospital in just a few days and are still very ill. These clients and their family members need skilled services and education about the disease process, prescribed medications, and future implications of their illnesses. Because so many home care clients have complex problems, nurses providing home care services must have all of the skills necessary to work in acute care, plus excellent communication and assessment skills.

Δ   Home health nurses provide a variety of skilled services, including, but not limited to:

•   Skilled assessment.

•   Wound care.

•   Laboratory draws.

•   Medication education and administration.

- Parenteral nutrition.

- IV fluids and medication.

- Central line care.

- Urinary catheter insertion and maintenance.

- Coordination/supervision of various other participants in health services.

Δ The home health nurse must evaluate the living environment for safety, paying close attention to loose rugs, electrical outlets and extension cords, the use of oxygen, and other environmental hazards. Because of the increased risk of falls for older adults within the home environment, pets, steep stairways, or a difficult bathroom set-up can all be safety issues. The nurse must evaluate these and other factors that could cause clients to fall or otherwise injure themselves. All of the following factors play an important role in the successful rehabilitation of the client; therefore, they must be taken into account by the home health nurse:

- Does the client have food in the house to eat?

- Is there help with household chores?

- Does the client live alone?

- Who is the client's support system?

- Is the client able to set up and dispense his own medication?

Δ Home health nurses often provide follow-up care after an acute hospital stay; therefore, they must educate the client and the family regarding complications or adverse reactions. These instructions may include when to contact the agency, the emergency room, or the primary care provider. Information and resources for families and clients can provide support in dealing with illness.

Δ By providing the client with education about his disease, the nurse encourages the client to be independent and to be involved in his own care. It also allows the family to be involved in the care and decision making regarding their family member. These advantages promote quality of life for clients and families by decreasing cost and reducing travel time (to and from the hospital).

Hospice Nurses

Δ Hospice nursing is a type of specialized home care. These services are for those clients deemed terminally ill. Clients who qualify for hospice usually have a prognosis of 6 months or less to live.

Δ The main goal of hospice is to provide quality of life to clients and their families during this end-of-life period.

Δ   Hospice nurses provide direct palliative care to clients in the form of pain management, symptom assessment and relief, comfort measures, and therapeutic communication.

Δ   Helping the family transition from an expectation of recovery to acceptance of death is a large aspect of providing hospice care. The hospice nurse may continue to work with the family for up to 1 year following the death of the client.

Occupational Health Nurses

Δ   The goal of occupational health is the health and safety of workers.

Δ   Occupational health nursing is focused on:

  • Assessing risks for work-related illness and injury.

  • Planning and delivery of health and safety services in the workplace.

  • Facilitation of health promotion activities that lead to a more productive workforce.

Δ   This autonomous specialty entails making independent nursing judgments when providing care to the workforce aggregate.

Δ   In assessing risk for work-related illness and injury, the nurse should keep in mind the following factors affecting susceptibility to illness and injury:

  • Host factors: worker characteristics, such as job inexperience, age, and pregnancy.

  • Agent factors: biological agents (viruses, bacteria, fungi, bloodborne and airborne pathogens); chemical agents (asbestos, smoke); mechanical agents (musculoskeletal or other strains from repetitive motions, poor workstation-worker fit, and lifting heavy loads); physical agents (temperature extremes, vibrations, noise, radiation, and lighting); and psychological agents (threats to psychological or social well-being resulting in work-related stress, burnout, and violence).

  • Environmental factors: physical factors (heat, odor, ventilation, pollution); social factors (sanitation, housing conditions, overcrowding, illiteracy); and psychological factors (addictions, stress).

Δ   Occupational health nurses' roles and responsibilities include:

  • Primary prevention – teaching good nutrition and knowledge of health hazards, identifying workplace hazards, and providing information on immunizations, use of protective equipment, and smoking cessation.

  • Secondary prevention – early detection through health surveillance and screening, prompt treatment, counseling and referral, and prevention of further limitations.

  • Tertiary prevention – restoration of health through rehabilitation strategies and limited duty programs.

Δ An occupational health history provides the framework for the nurse to begin to assess the worker for possible exposure to health hazards. The goal is to identify agents and host factors that place the worker at risk and to identify ways to eliminate or minimize exposure and prevent potential health problems. Information elicited should include:

   • Current and past jobs.

   • Current and past exposure to specific agents and any relationship of current symptoms to work activities.

   • Any precipitating factors, such as underlying illness, previous injuries, and healthy and unhealthy habits.

Δ A worksite walk-through or survey is also part of a workplace assessment. Focus should be given to observation of work processes and materials, job requirements, actual and potential hazards, employee work practices (e.g., hygiene, waste disposal, housekeeping), the incidence/prevalence of work-related illness/injuries, and control strategies to eliminate exposures.

Δ Control strategies are designed to reduce future exposures based upon results from investigations into work-related illness/injury. Control strategies often include engineering, altering work practices, providing personal protective equipment and education to prevent future injuries, workplace monitoring, health screening, employee-assistance programs, job-task analysis and design, risk management, and emergency preparedness.

Δ Protection from violence – Work can be frustrating and can contribute to stress, resulting in aggression and violence against another. Being aware of jobs that are repetitive, boring, or physically and psychologically draining can help to identify workers who, as a result, may feel tired, angry, and generally inadequate. Nurses can refer such workers to employee-assistance programs that provide confidential counseling and referrals to other professional services if needed.

Δ Protection from work-related injuries from falls, environmental hazards, and burns – Nurses can use research and trend analysis to improve working conditions by eliminating or minimizing hazards and potential problems. Additional strategies include providing safety and health education programs to workers, developing health policy focused on ensuring effective employee health and safety, designing strategies to prevent work-related accidents/injuries, keeping abreast of Occupational Health and Safety Administration (OSHA) standards and resource programs, and working to influence legislation aimed at workers/workplace health protection.

School Nurses

Δ   School nursing encompasses many roles:

- Case manager: Ensures the provision and evaluation of comprehensive school-based health services and other related services for the children.

- Community outreach: Strives to meet the needs of all school-age children by cooperative planning and collaboration between the educational system and other community agencies.

- Consultant: Assists students, families, and personnel in information gathering and decision making about a variety of health needs and resources.

- Counselor: Supports students on a wide variety of health needs.

- Direct caregiver: Provides nursing care to ill or injured children at school.

- Health educator: Helps prepare children, families, school personnel, and the community to make well-informed health decisions.

- Researcher: Contributes to the base of knowledge for school health and educational needs.

Δ   The community health nurse working with school-age children should use a well-organized, comprehensive school health program that considers the developmental needs and characteristics of children. Key components of a comprehensive school health program include health education, physical education, health services, nutrition services, counseling, psychological and social services, promotion of a healthy school environment, health promotion for staff, and facilitation of family/community involvement.

Components of Comprehensive School Health Programs	
Component	Description
Health education	Teaching children concepts of health
Physical education	Promoting physical activity in school
Health services	Providing health services in school at an appropriate nurse-to-student ratio (e.g., 1:750)
Nutrition services	Teaching nutrition and diet concepts and providing breakfast and lunch for children who qualify by federal standards
Counseling, psychological, and social services	Promoting health of children with special needs, including those who receive special education services through the Individuals with Disabilities Act (IDEA)
Promotion of a healthy school environment	Reducing tobacco use and violence in schools
Health promotion for staff	Providing health care for school teachers and staff
Facilitation of family/community involvement	Promoting health services in the community

Primary Prevention in the Schools		
Assessments	NANDA Nursing Diagnoses	Examples of Nursing Interventions
The school nurse assesses the knowledge base of the children regarding health issues.	• Deficient knowledge • Health-seeking behaviors	The nurse teaches children health promotion including: • Handwashing and tooth-brushing. • Healthy food choices. • Chronic disease risk reduction. • Prevention of childhood injuries (e.g., bicycle safety). • Substance abuse prevention.
The school nurse is required by law to maintain complete records on the immunization status of children.	Risk for infection	Certain immunizations are required for all children in the school (state-mandated). Examples include: • DTaP (diphtheria, tetanus, pertussis series). • MMR (measles, mumps, rubella). • Polio.

Secondary Prevention in the Schools		
Assessments	NANDA Nursing Diagnoses	Examples of Nursing Interventions
The school nurse must assess children who become ill or who are injured at school.	Diagnoses are illness-related. • Acute pain • Nausea • Impaired skin integrity	The nurse provides care to children with: • Headaches. • Stomach pain. • Injuries that occur at school. The nurse uses *Standard Precautions* at all times.
The school nurse needs to assess children, faculty, staff, and the situation when a health emergency occurs.	Ineffective health maintenance	The school nurse provides emergency care including: • First aid. • CPR. Emergency plans drawn up in the school should be followed. The nurse's responsibility is to maintain a fully supplied clinic office.

Secondary Prevention in the Schools		
Assessments	**NANDA Nursing Diagnoses**	**Examples of Nursing Interventions**
The school nurse assesses children who require medication administration in the schools.	• Self-care deficit • Ineffective therapeutic regimen management	• The school nurse is responsible for administering medication per the primary care provider's prescription. • The prescribed medication should be in the original bottle and be stored in a secure place. • Written consent by the parents is required.
The school nurse assesses children as they are screened for early detection of disease.	• Health-seeking behaviors • Readiness for enhanced nutrition	Depending on state law, the school nurse screens children to detect disease: • Vision and hearing. • Height and weight. • Oral health. • Scoliosis. • Lice. • General physical examinations.
The school nurse assesses children to detect child abuse or neglect.	Risk for violence	The school nurse is required by state law to officially report all suspected cases of child abuse/neglect.
The school nurse must assess children for evidence of mental illness, suicide, and violence.	• Risk for violence • Risk for self-directed violence • Risk for suicide	• The school nurse should educate teachers and staff about risk factors related to suicide in children. • Violence in schools can be reduced by nurses providing health education and follow-up for at-risk children.
The school nurse assesses disaster situations.	Ineffective coping (community)	The nurse provides triage and care during and after a school crisis: • Natural disasters. • Community crises.

Tertiary Prevention in the Schools		
Assessments	NANDA Nursing Diagnoses	Examples of Nursing Interventions
The school nurse participates in developing the individual education plan (IEP) for children with disabilities.	Risk for delayed development	The school nurse works with the child/family to achieve a long-term outcome of increased attendance for a child with autism.
The school nurse assesses children with long-term health needs at school.	Ineffective health maintenance	The school nurse provides nursing care for children at school who have: • Asthma. • Diabetes mellitus. • Cystic fibrosis. The school nurse provides care at school to children who have specific health needs, including: • Urinary catheterizations. • Dressing changes. • IV line monitoring.

Parish Nurses

Δ Parish nursing promotes the health and wellness of populations of faith communities. The population often includes church members and individuals and groups in the geographical community.

Δ Parish nurses work closely with pastoral care staff, professional health care members, and lay volunteers to provide a holistic approach to healing (body, mind, and spirit).

Δ Confidentiality is essential in parish nursing practice.

Δ Functions of the parish nurse include:

• Personal health counseling (health-risk appraisals, spiritual assessments, support for numerous acute and chronic, actual and potential health problems).

• Health education (available resources, classes, individual and group teaching).

• Liaison between faith community and local resources.

• Facilitator (support groups, change within the parish, volunteer training).

• Spiritual support (help identify spiritual strengths for coping).

Case Managers

Δ   Case management nursing includes:

- Promoting interdisciplinary services and increased client/family involvement.
- Decreasing cost by improving client outcomes.
- Providing education to optimize health participation.

Δ   Collaboration between clients, family, community resources, payer sources, and other health care professionals contributes to successful management of the client's health care needs. Sometimes the greatest role the case manager plays is in advocating for the client to obtain necessary treatments or community support.

Δ   Case management nurses must possess excellent communication skills in order to facilitate communication among all parties involved. Being able to articulate the needs of the client to various parties can save time and unnecessary distress.

Δ   Utilizing the nursing process during case management will also help the client to obtain important services and to treat his condition.

Assessment	• Clarify the problem by evaluating physical needs, psychosocial issues, functional ability, and financial constraints. • Determine the cause and precipitating factors.
Diagnosis	Identify applicable nursing diagnoses by using the above assessment.
Planning	In conjunction with the client and the family, determine: • Possible outcomes for the client. • Advantages and disadvantages of possible outcomes. • What role each participant will play. • Impact on the client in each of the areas listed for the assessment.
Intervention	The case manager: • Contacts service providers. • Provides referral information. • Coordinates all services to be provided. • Monitors the client to determine if services are still appropriate.
Evaluation (continued monitoring)	Monitor the care provided by the different agencies, comparing against: • Original projected outcomes. • Physical needs. • Psychosocial needs. • Financial needs. • Client and family satisfaction.

Δ   Because case management is not well understood, the success of these programs has been limited. For a nurse to function in this role, she must be a team player who provides a link between all facets of the health care experience. This means coordinating care between the primary care providers, nursing staff, physical and occupational therapists, rehabilitation facilities, and home health care. The case manager must be proactive for the client, balancing the impact of the illness against the cost of care.

Δ   Although little research exists, successful case management should be able to improve continuity of care, decrease hospital stays, and promote client satisfaction. By empowering clients and involving them in their own care, case managers effectively improve the client outcomes. Increased knowledge and awareness of the disease process will decrease hospital stays because of early intervention. Utilization of appropriate community agencies will also contain costs, as the monitoring of clients leads to better disease management.

Δ   Case management has a positive impact on client health care by creating a liaison for the client to the health care system. Advocating for clients, keeping them involved in the process, and informing them about their health care will result in improved outcomes for all involved.

Primary Reference:

Stanhope, M., & Lancaster, J. (2006). *Foundations of nursing in the community: Community-oriented practice* (2nd ed.). St. Louis, MO: Mosby.

Additional Resources:

NANDA International (2004). *NANDA nursing diagnoses: Definitions and classification 2005-2006*. Philadelphia: NANDA.

Chapter 10: Roles and Settings in Community Health Nursing

Application Exercises

Scenario: A nurse is caring for a 56-year-old man with diabetes mellitus and end-stage renal disease. He has been insulin dependent for many years. He is currently receiving home care services for a foot ulcer that is not healing. His primary care provider has prescribed dialysis.

1. Identify the services that this client could receive at home. Who should coordinate those services?

2. What psychosocial nursing diagnoses might be applicable to this client?

3. What teaching should the nurse provide to the client/primary caregiver to help the client stay out of the hospital?

4. When would this client move from home care to hospice? How would the nursing care be different?

5. The philosophy of hospice care includes which of the following?

        A. Provide the client with all life-sustaining measures.

        B. All diseases can be cured.

        C. Provide support for clients and families during the dying process.

        D. Provide pain management only.

6. Which of the following clients are eligible to receive home care services? (Select all that apply.)

     _____ Homebound older adult client

     _____ Terminally ill child

     _____ Individuals dependent on health care technology (e.g., ventilator)

     _____ Postoperative clients

7. A nurse is completing an occupational health history on a worker. What questions should the nurse include?

8. What elements should be included in a worksite assessment?

9. Which of the following workers is most prone to having a work-related accident?

        A. 25-year-old male working in his third year in sales

        B. 29-year-old pregnant postal service worker

        C. 45-year-old female grocery clerk

        D. 30-year-old male college professor

Scenario: A nurse has just started a new job as a school nurse. The school board has asked her to evaluate the school health program and to suggest areas for improvement. When assessing the school health program, the nurse discovers the following:

There is one school nurse for every 1,000 students.
There is no wellness program for faculty and staff.
The school is free of environmental hazards.
There is no medication administration policy in place.
The school works with a neighboring hospital and provides students with health care through a collaborative volunteer program.
Complete clinical services are available at the school-based clinic during school hours.
Physical education classes are offered twice a week for all students.
The school provides a nutritionally balanced breakfast and lunch program.
The school employs a full-time counselor.
Health education that is planned is provided for students at each grade level by the school nurse.
The school is a smoke-free environment.
Two children who use wheelchairs are tutored at home and do not attend classes at the school.

10. What strengths and weaknesses are present in the school health program?

11. Which weakness in the school health program is the highest in priority and requires immediate change? Why?

Scenario: A case manager is assigned the case of a 12-year-old boy who has recently been diagnosed with diabetes mellitus. He attends middle school and is in the 7th grade. He is unreceptive to learning about his disease and does not want to learn to read the glucometer or to give his own insulin shots. Although he has learned some about diet, he still eats what he wants, when he wants, without regard for his physical condition or blood sugar.

12. What communication techniques and approach should the case manager employ?

13. In this situation, who needs education? (Select all that apply.)

_____ The client
_____ His parents and siblings
_____ His classmates
_____ The school teacher

14. List some techniques to help the client take responsibility for his diabetes monitoring and treatment.

15. Which of the following would help to keep this child from feeling alone with regard to his diabetes?

A. Attend a diabetic camp for preteens.
B. Attend a diabetic support group of all ages.
C. Encourage the school nurse to meet and talk with him about diabetes.
D. Let his parents home school him.

16. Considering his age group, which of the following is the best educational tool for this client?

A. A book to read about diabetes
B. A video game about diabetes
C. Attending a lecture on diabetes
D. Getting his information from his friends at school

Chapter 10: Roles and Settings in Community Health Nursing

Application Exercises Answer Key

Scenario: A nurse is caring for a 56-year-old man with diabetes mellitus and end-stage renal disease. He has been insulin dependent for many years. He is currently receiving home care services for a foot ulcer that is not healing. His primary care provider has prescribed dialysis.

1. Identify the services that this client could receive at home. Who should coordinate those services?

   The case manager should coordinate services that the client could receive at home, including:

   > **Nursing care to help with dressing changes and wound monitoring.**
   > **Physical therapist to direct strengthening exercises, increasing mobility and circulation.**
   > **Occupational therapist to evaluate the environment for potential hazards (e.g., rugs) and any need for handrails or other assistive devices.**
   > **Dietary consult for instruction regarding a low-phosphorus, high-protein diet.**
   > **Social worker to assist with paperwork, referral to community resources, and the possible need to set up transportation to dialysis.**

2. What psychosocial nursing diagnoses might be applicable to this client?

   > **Ineffective coping**
   > **Interrupted family process**
   > **Deficient knowledge**
   > **Impaired social interaction**

3. What teaching should the nurse provide to the client/primary caregiver to help the client stay out of the hospital?

   > **Signs and symptoms of infection**
   > **Education regarding diabetes, including blood glucose monitoring, insulin injections, diet, and exercise**
   > **Education about end-stage renal disease and dialysis**
   > **Consultation with dietitian**

4. When would this client move from home care to hospice? How would the nursing care be different?

The client should be moved to hospice at the point when his disease is determined to be terminal. If he decides to refuse dialysis, or dialysis is not successful in regulating his electrolytes, then he may be determined to only have 6 months to live. When a client moves from home care to hospice, life-saving measures are no longer pursued. The goal becomes quality of life at the end of life. Pain management and symptom control become the foci of care.

5. The philosophy of hospice care includes which of the following?

        A. Provide the client with all life-sustaining measures.

        B. All diseases can be cured.

        C. Provide support for clients and families during the dying process.

        D. Provide pain management only.

The philosophy of hospice is to provide palliative care to terminally ill clients.

6. Which of the following clients are eligible to receive home care services? (Select all that apply.)

      _X_   Homebound older adult client

      _X_   Terminally ill child

      _X_   Individuals dependent on health care technology (e.g., ventilator)

      _____   Postoperative clients

Homebound older adult clients, terminally ill children, and individuals dependent on health care technology are eligible to receive home care services. A routine postoperative client would not, unless specific needs were identified (e.g., enteral feedings).

7. A nurse is completing an occupational health history on a worker. What questions should the nurse include?

What type of work do you do?
What potential exposures have you experienced?
To what processes and operations, raw materials, by-products are you exposed?
What is your work environment like (e.g., general conditions, safety signs and precautions, physical environment, cleanliness, ventilation)?
What work-related illnesses/injuries have you had?
What is your average number of days missed per year and the reasons for those absences?
What types of uniforms, clothing do you wear? How is it laundered?

8. What elements should be included in a worksite assessment?

The work, work processes, and related hazards, products, and exposures
Work environment (cleanliness, clutter, ventilation, noise, temperature, lighting, safety, signs, waste disposal mechanisms)
Worker population characteristics
Staffing and personnel
Corporate culture
Written policies/procedures for occupational health care
Most common illnesses/injuries
Health promotion programs
Regulatory compliance with OSHA standards

9. Which of the following workers is most prone to having a work-related accident?

A. 25-year-old male working in his third year in sales
B. 29-year-old pregnant postal service worker
C. 45-year-old female grocery clerk
D. 30-year-old male college professor

Worker characteristics such as job inexperience, age, and pregnancy increase risk for work-related injuries.

Scenario: A nurse has just started a new job as a school nurse. The school board has asked her to evaluate the school health program and to suggest areas for improvement. When assessing the school health program, the nurse discovers the following:

> There is one school nurse for every 1,000 students.
> There is no wellness program for faculty and staff.
> The school is free of environmental hazards.
> There is no medication administration policy in place.
> The school works with a neighboring hospital and provides students with health care through a collaborative volunteer program.
> Complete clinical services are available at the school-based clinic during school hours.
> Physical education classes are offered twice a week for all students.
> The school provides a nutritionally balanced breakfast and lunch program.
> The school employs a full-time counselor.
> Health education that is planned is provided for students at each grade level by the school nurse.
> The school is a smoke-free environment.
> Two children who use wheelchairs are tutored at home and do not attend classes at the school.

10. What strengths and weaknesses are present in the school health program?

Strengths:

> **School is free of hazards and is smoke free.**
> **There is collaboration with community agencies for health care.**
> **Complete health services are available at the school, including a school counselor.**
> **Physical education is provided at school.**
> **Nutrition programs are in place for students.**
> **Health education is given to students.**

Weaknesses:

> **There is no medication administration policy.**
> **There is no health promotion program for the staff.**
> **The nurse-to-student ratio is too high.**
> **Children with chronic illnesses are excluded from school.**

11. Which weakness in the school health program is the highest in priority and requires immediate change? Why?

The greatest weakness is the lack of a medication administration policy. In order to comply with federal and state laws that protect children, a policy should be developed immediately to safeguard the children who receive medication in the schools.

Scenario: A case manager is assigned the case of a 12-year-old boy who has recently been diagnosed with diabetes mellitus. He attends middle school and is in the 7th grade. He is unreceptive to learning about his disease and does not want to learn to read the glucometer or to give his own insulin shots. Although he has learned some about diet, he still eats what he wants, when he wants, without regard for his physical condition or blood sugar.

12. What communication techniques and approach should the case manager employ?

Try to reach the client at his level. Have him practice with the glucometer in a nonthreatening environment. Let him meet kids his own age that have been successful in monitoring and treating their diabetes. Show him some Internet resources for preteens on diabetes.

13. In this situation, who needs education? (Select all that apply.)

__X__ The client
__X__ His parents and siblings
__X__ His classmates
__X__ The school teacher

The more people who understand the situation, the easier it will be for the client to be compliant. Children at this age are very worried about what their peers think, so it is important for the teacher and his friends at school to be supportive of his measures to be proactive in caring for his diabetes.

14. List some techniques to help the client take responsibility for his diabetes monitoring and treatment.

Education provides power, and there is a need to empower this client. Make him the expert on diabetes by providing information in a fun and informative way. Check the Internet for Web sites where he can "chat" with other preteens who have diabetes and learn what they do to manage their diabetes. Get him involved in a preteen diabetic support group. Part of this client's regimen will need to include feeling that he belongs to a group.

15. Which of the following would help to keep this child from feeling alone with regard to his diabetes?

A. Attend a diabetic camp for preteens.

B. Attend a diabetic support group of all ages.

C. Encourage the school nurse to meet and talk with him about diabetes.

D. Let his parents home school him.

The more fun he has while learning, the more the client will learn. Diabetic camps that are geared for age groups teach clients how to manage their disease while still enjoying a "normal" life. That's important for clients in this (and any) age group.

16. Considering his age group, which of the following is the best educational tool for this client?

A. A book to read about diabetes

B. A video game about diabetes

C. Attending a lecture on diabetes

D. Getting his information from his friends at school

Video games and preteens go together well. Let the client play a video game that will be fun and educational. This will increase his understanding of his disease process.

Chapter 11:   Nursing Care of Aggregates in the Community
Contributor: Sharon Lytle, MS, RN, CNM

 Learning Objectives:

Δ   Discuss health concerns/leading causes of death, screening/preventive services, *Healthy People 2010* initiatives, and community education foci in caring for community aggregates of children and adolescents.

Δ   Discuss health concerns/leading causes of death, screening/preventive services, *Healthy People 2010* initiatives, and community education foci in caring for community aggregates of women.

Δ   Discuss health concerns/leading causes of death, screening/preventive services, *Healthy People 2010* initiatives, and community education foci in caring for community aggregates of men.

Δ   Discuss health concerns/leading causes of death, screening/preventive services, *Healthy People 2010* initiatives, and community education foci in caring for community aggregates of older adults.

Δ   Discuss the role of community health nurses in the assessment and promotion of the health of families within a community and the *Healthy People 2010* initiatives related to family health.

Children (Birth to 10 Years) and Adolescents

Δ   **Health Concerns/Leading Causes of Death**

• Children

◊   Perinatal conditions/congenital anomalies

◊   Sudden Infant Death Syndrome (SIDS)

◊   Motor vehicle/other unintentional injuries

• Adolescents

◊   Motor vehicle/other unintentional injuries

◊   Homicide

◊   Suicide

Δ   **Screening/Preventive Services**

- Children

  ◊   Height/weight

  ◊   Vision

  ◊   At birth: hemoglobinopathy, phenylalanine level, T_4 and TSH

  ◊   Immunization status – check the Centers for Disease Control and Prevention (CDC) Web site, *www.cdc.gov*, for current administration schedules

  ◊   Dental health

- Adolescents

  ◊   Height/weight

  ◊   Dental health

  ◊   Papanicolaou (Pap) smear test (females)

  ◊   Chlamydia screen (females)

  ◊   Rubella serology/vaccination history (females)

  ◊   Substance abuse

  ◊   Immunization status (*www.cdc.gov*)

Δ   *Healthy People 2010* **Initiatives**

- Children and Adolescents

  ◊   Reductions in:

  ○   Childhood obesity

  ○   Exposure to smoke

  ◊   Increases in:

  ○   Immunizations

  ○   Use of child restraints

  ○   Physical education in schools

  ○   Lead-based paint testing

  ○   Asthma care

Δ   **Community Education**

- Children

  ◊   Breastfeeding

  ◊   Sleeping positions

  ◊   Nutrition

- ◊ Physical activity
- ◊ Substance use
- ◊ Dental hygiene/health
- ◊ Skin protection
- ◊ Injury prevention
- ◊ Car safety
- ◊ Helmet use
- ◊ Fire safety
- ◊ Poison control
- ◊ CPR training
- ◊ Water safety
- Adolescents
  - ◊ Substance use
  - ◊ Sexual behavior
  - ◊ Nutrition, especially calcium intake for females
  - ◊ Exercise
  - ◊ Skin protection
  - ◊ Injury prevention
    - ° Car safety
    - ° Fire safety
    - ° Firearm safety

Women

Δ **Health Concerns/Leading Causes of Death**

- Reproductive health
- Menopause
- Osteoporosis
- Heart disease
- Diabetes mellitus
- Malignant neoplasm (breast, cervical, ovarian, colorectal)

Δ **Screening/Preventive Services**

- Height/weight
- Blood pressure

- Cholesterol (ages 45-64)

- Dental health

- Pap smear test

- Mammogram/clinical breast exam

- Fecal occult blood test/sigmoidoscopy (≥ 50 years)

- Rubella serology/vaccination history (childbearing years)

- Immunization status – check the CDC Web site, *www.cdc.gov*, for current administration schedules

- Diabetes mellitus

- HIV

- Skin cancer

Δ *Healthy People 2010* **Initiatives**

- Reductions in:

  ◊ Osteoporosis

  ◊ Breast cancer deaths

  ◊ Rape

- Increases in:

  ◊ Proportion of intended pregnancies

  ◊ Percentage who receive early/adequate prenatal care

  ◊ Breastfeeding rates

  ◊ Proportion of adults who are aware of early warning symptoms of heart attack and access rapid emergency care

Δ **Community Education**

- Nutrition

- STD prevention

- Substance use

- Breast self-examination

- Skin protection

- HIV prevention

- Injury prevention

  ◊ Car safety

  ◊ Fire safety

  ◊ Violence

Men

Δ **Health Concerns/Leading Causes of Death**

- Heart disease

- Malignant neoplasm (prostate, testicular, skin, colorectal)

- Accidents

- Lung disease

- Liver disease

Δ **Screening/Preventive Services**

- Height/weight

- Blood pressure

- Dental health

- Digital rectal exam

- Fecal occult blood test/sigmoidoscopy (≥ 50 years)

- Immunization status – check the CDC Web site, *www.cdc.gov*, for current administration schedules

- Diabetes mellitus

- HIV

- Skin cancer

- Cholesterol (ages 35-64 years)

Δ *Healthy People 2010* **Initiatives**

- Reductions in:

  ◊ Prostate cancer death rate

  ◊ New AIDS cases

  ◊ Intentional injuries resulting from alcohol- and illicit-drug-related violence

- Increases in:

  ◊ Male involvement in pregnancy prevention/family planning

  ◊ Proportion of adults who are aware of early warning symptoms of heart attack and access rapid emergency care

Δ **Community Education**

- Nutrition

- Self-testicular exam

- Skin protection

- Substance use

- HIV prevention

- Injury prevention

  ◊ Car safety

  ◊ Fire safety

  ◊ Firearm safety

  ◊ Violence

Older Adults

Δ **Health Concerns/Leading Causes of Death**

- Heart disease

- Malignant neoplasm

- Cerebrovascular disease

- Chronic obstructive pulmonary disease

- Pneumonia and influenza

Δ **Screening/Preventive Services**

- Blood pressure

- Height/weight

- Dental health

- Fecal occult blood test/sigmoidoscopy

- Mammogram/clinical breast exam (women)

- Pap smear test (women)

- Vision

- Hearing

- Substance abuse

- Immunization status (pneumococcal, influenza) – check the CDC Web site, *www.cdc.gov*, for current administration schedules

- Functional assessment (self-care abilities)

- Medication history

- Osteoporosis

- Diabetes mellitus

- Skin cancer

Δ   *Healthy People 2010* **Initiatives**

- Reductions in:

  ◊   Proportion of adults with chronic joint symptoms

  ◊   Proportion of adults who are hospitalized for vertebral fractures associated with osteoporosis

  ◊   Proportion of adults with disabilities who suffer depression

  ◊   Hospitalizations due to heart failure

  ◊   Tobacco use by older adults

  ◊   Visual impairment due to cataract

- Increases in:

  ◊   Medication review by health care providers

  ◊   Proportion of adults who exercise to maintain muscular strength and endurance

Δ   **Community Education**

- Substance use

- Nutrition

- Exercise

- Dental health

- Sexual behavior

- Injury prevention

  ◊   Car safety

  ◊   Fall prevention

  ◊   Fire safety

  ◊   CPR training (household members)

  ◊   Violence

Families

Δ   The family as client is basic to community-oriented nursing practice. Community health nurses have a significant role to play in promoting healthy families.

Δ   Community health nurses must engage in community assessment, planning, development, and evaluation activities that are focused on family issues.

Δ   Home visits provide community health nurses with the opportunity to observe the home environment and to identify barriers and supports to health-risk reduction.

Δ   Family crisis occurs when a family is not able to cope with an event. The family's resources are inadequate for the demands of the situation.

Δ   Transitions are times of risk for families. Transitions include birth or adoption of a child, death of a family member, child moving out of the home, marriage of a child, major illness, divorce, and loss of the main family income. These transitions require families to change behaviors, make new decisions, reallocate family roles, learn new skills, and learn to use new resources.

Δ   **Characteristics of Healthy Families**

- Members communicate well and listen to each other.

- There is affirmation and support for all members.

- Members teach respect for others.

- There is a sense of trust.

- Members play and share humor together.

- Members interact with one another.

- There is a shared sense of responsibility.

- There are traditions and rituals.

- Members seek help for their problems.

Δ   **Family Health Risk Appraisal**

- Biological health risk assessment: Genograms are used to gather basic information about the family, relationships within the family, and health and illness patterns. Repetitions of diseases with a genetic component (e.g., cancer, heart disease, diabetes mellitus) can be identified.

- Environmental risk: Ecomaps are used to identify family interactions with other groups and organizations. Information about the family's support network and social risk is gathered.

- Behavioral risk: Information is gathered about the family's health behavior, including health values, health habits, and health risk perceptions.

Δ   ***Healthy People 2010* Initiatives**

- Reductions in:
    ◊   Proportion of families that experience difficulties in obtaining health care services

    ◊   Indoor allergen levels

    ◊   Proportion of families whose ability to conceive or maintain a pregnancy is impaired

    ◊   Proportion of children who are regularly exposed to tobacco smoke at home

- Increases in:
    ◊   Proportion of health care organizations that provide client and family education

    ◊   Proportion of persons who live in homes tested for radon

    ◊   Food security among U.S. households, thereby decreasing hunger

Primary Reference:

Stanhope, M., & Lancaster, J. (2006). *Foundations of nursing in the community: Community-oriented practice* (2nd ed.). St. Louis, MO: Mosby.

Chapter 11: Nursing Care of Aggregates in the Community

Application Exercises

Scenario: A client presents to the community health clinic for a free mammogram and Pap smear. She is a 45-year-old Hispanic female and has not received health care of any kind since the birth of her youngest child, who is now 10 years old. She was just hired for full-time employment and is in need of a complete physical examination as required for the position. The medical history provided by the client is unremarkable. She has no documentation of immunizations from her childhood in Mexico. She is positive that she had Varicella as a child. She reports five spontaneous vaginal deliveries. Her husband of 25 years died 6 months ago.

1. Identify the health screenings that are recommended for this client.

2. Consulting current immunization schedules (*www.cdc.gov*), identify which specific immunizations are recommended for this client.

Scenario: A wellness screening and educational program is being offered at a local senior center in the Midwest during the month of October. The focus of the screening is on health promotion during the winter months.

3. Identify what immunizations should be offered.

4. Identify some topics that should be considered for inclusion in the educational program.

Chapter 11: Nursing Care of Aggregates in the Community

Application Exercises Answer Key

Scenario: A client presents to the community health clinic for a free mammogram and Pap smear. She is a 45-year-old Hispanic female and has not received health care of any kind since the birth of her youngest child, who is now 10 years old. She was just hired for full-time employment and is in need of a complete physical examination as required for the position. The medical history provided by the client is unremarkable. She has no documentation of immunizations from her childhood in Mexico. She is positive that she had Varicella as a child. She reports five spontaneous vaginal deliveries. Her husband of 25 years died 6 months ago.

1. Identify the health screenings that are recommended for this client.

   Height
   Weight
   Blood pressure
   Total blood cholesterol
   Immunization status
   Pap smear test
   Baseline mammogram and clinical breast exam
   Substance abuse
   Dental health

2. Consulting current immunization schedules (*www.cdc.gov*), identify which specific immunizations are recommended for this client.

   Tetanus-diphtheria (Td): boosters every 10 years
   Poliovirus vaccine
   Influenza vaccine
   MMR
   Hepatitis A and B vaccines

Scenario: A wellness screening and educational program is being offered at a local senior center in the Midwest during the month of October. The focus of the screening is on health promotion during the winter months.

3. Identify what immunizations should be offered.

Along with immunization updates (e.g., pneumococcal, Td), influenza vaccines are recommended annually between October and November.

4. Identify some topics that should be considered for inclusion in the educational program.

Prevention of falls, particularly related to weather conditions
Importance of influenza vaccines
Weather-related issues (e.g., staying warm, driving precautions)
Other general topics: nutrition, home safety, medication safety

Chapter 12:   Special Community Needs

Contributor: Angeline Bushy, PhD, RN, FAAN
Carel Mountain, MSN, RN

 Learning Objectives:

Δ   Discuss the community health nurse's role in meeting special community needs, including violence and abuse, substance abuse, mental illness, and homelessness.

Δ   Discuss the community health nurse's role in promoting health in rural and migrant populations.

Δ   Discuss the community health nurse's role in promoting environmental health.

Violence and Abuse

Δ   Types of Violence Within Communities

- Homicide

    ◊   When committed by strangers, homicide is often related to a substance abuse network.

    ◊   Most homicides are committed by a friend, acquaintance, or family member during an argument.

    ◊   Within families, homicide is often preceded by abuse of a family member.

    ◊   Rates are increasing among adolescents.

- Assault

    ◊   Males are more likely to be assaulted.

    ◊   Youths are at a significantly higher risk.

- Rape

    ◊   Rape is often unreported.

    ◊   It includes date and marital rape.

    ◊   The majority of violence against women is intimate partner violence.

    ◊   There is an increased incidence reported in cities between the hours of 8 p.m. and 2 a.m., on weekends, and in the summer.

- Suicide
  - ◊ More suicide attempts are reported for women.
  - ◊ Males are more likely to die from suicide.
  - ◊ Male adolescents, ages 15-19, are more likely to commit suicide than females of the same age range.
- Sexual abuse
  - ◊ Female children are more likely to be sexually abused than male children.
- Physical abuse
- Emotional abuse
- Neglect

Δ Individual Assessment

- Factors influencing an individual's potential for violence
  - ◊ History of being abused or exposure to violence
  - ◊ Low self-esteem
  - ◊ Fear and distrust of others
  - ◊ Poor self-control
  - ◊ Inadequate social skills
  - ◊ Immature motivation for marriage or childbearing
  - ◊ Weak coping skills
- Recognizing actual or potential child abuse
  - ◊ Unexplained injury
  - ◊ Unusual fear of the nurse and others
  - ◊ Evidence of injuries not mentioned in history (e.g., old burns, scars, ecchymosis, human bite marks)
  - ◊ Fractures, including older healed fractures
  - ◊ Subdural hematomas
  - ◊ Trauma to genitalia
  - ◊ Malnourishment or dehydration
  - ◊ General poor hygiene or inappropriate dress for weather conditions
  - ◊ Considered to be a "bad child"

Δ   Recognizing potential or actual older adult abuse

- ◊   Unexplained or repeated physical injuries
- ◊   Physical neglect and unmet basic needs
- ◊   Rejection of assistance by caregiver
- ◊   Financial mismanagement
- ◊   Withdrawal and passivity
- ◊   Depression

Δ   Community Assessment: Social and Community Factors Influencing Violence

- Work stress
- Unemployment
- Media exposure to violence
- Crowded living conditions
- Poverty
- Feelings of powerlessness
- Social isolation
- Lack of community resources (e.g., playgrounds, parks, theaters)

Δ   Strategies to Reduce Societal Violence

- Primary prevention
  - ◊   The focus is on:
    - ° Stopping the cycle of abuse by teaching and supporting persons who have experienced abuse in the past.
    - ° Nonviolent conflict resolution and anger management.
    - ° Increasing abilities to deal with stress and to eliminate or reduce factors that contribute to stress.
  - ◊   Examples of primary prevention include:
    - ° Teach alternative methods of conflict resolution, anger management, and coping strategies in schools or community centers and after-school programs.
    - ° Organize parenting classes to assist families in developing effective parent-child and intimate partner relationships by assisting with communication and anticipatory guidance of expected age-appropriate behaviors. Teach new parents and parents of school-age children about appropriate parental responses and forms of discipline. This can be done at parent group meetings, childbirth classes, high school parenting classes, or during home visits for Healthy Start programs.

- Educate citizens about the problem of violence, potential causes of violence, and the community services that are available to serve those in need.

- Promote public understanding about the aging process and about safeguards to ensure a safe and secure environment for older adults in the community.

- Assist in removing or reducing factors that contribute to stress by referring caretakers of older adult clients to respite services, assisting an unemployed parent in finding employment, or increasing social support networks for socially isolated families.

- Encourage older adults and their families to safeguard their funds and property by getting more information about a financial representative trust, durable power of attorney, a representative payee, and joint tenancy.

- Teach individuals that no one has a right to touch or hurt another person, and make sure they know how to report cases of abuse.

- Secondary prevention
  - The focus is on:
    - Early identification, diagnosis, and treatment of abuse.
    - Screening of those at risk for abuse and of individuals who are potential abusers.
    - The safety of all involved.
  - Privacy and confidentiality must be respected.
  - Includes provision of around-the-clock and emergency services for treatment and temporary shelter.
  - Examples of secondary prevention include:
    - Assess and evaluate any unexplained bruises or injuries of any individual.
    - Screen all pregnant women for potential abuse. This may be the one time in a woman's life that she may access the health care system on a regular basis.
    - Build trust and confidence with a client.
    - If a violent situation exists, assess for immediate danger, provide appropriate care for the consequences of violence, develop a plan for safety, make needed referrals for community services and legal options, and refer to community shelters and programs.
    - If abuse has occurred, fully and completely record what is actually observed and refrain from opinions and interpretations. Complete mandatory reporting of suspected child abuse and, if required, report spousal violence or senior abuse. Follow a telephone report with a written report, usually within 48 hr.

- Refer sexual assault or rape victims to a local emergency department for assessment by a sexual assault abuse team. Caution the client not to bathe following the assault, as this destroys physical evidence.

- Assess and counsel any person contemplating suicide or homicide and refer the individual to the appropriate services.

- Support and educate the offender, even though a report must be made.

- Assess and help offenders address and deal with the stressors that may be causing or contributing to the abuse, such as mental illness or substance abuse.

- Alert all involved about available resources within the community.

- Tertiary prevention

  ◊ The focus is on:

  - Dealing with the consequences of violence and prevention of reoccurrence.

  - Rehabilitative services.

  - Empowering clients to have the strength to change conditions and to gain control of their situations.

  ◊ Includes the treatment of adults who were abused as children.

  ◊ Establishes parameters for long-term follow-up and supervision.

  ◊ Examples of tertiary prevention include:

  - When dealing with victims of abuse, develop a trusting relationship and focus on the client, not the situation.

  - Make resources in the community available to the client (e.g., telephone numbers of crisis lines and shelters).

  - If court systems are involved, work with parents while the child is out of the home (e.g., in foster care).

  - Refer to mental health professionals for long-term assistance.

  - Provide grief counseling to families of suicide or homicide victims.

  - Develop support groups for caregivers and victims of violence.

  - Advocate for legislation designed to assist older adult independence and caregivers and to increase funding for programs that supply services to low-income, at-risk communities.

Substance Abuse

Δ   Substance abuse is the use of any substance (including legal and prescribed) that threatens an individual's health or social and economic functioning.

Δ   Substance abuse affects all family members and often produces codependency in the nonaddicted individuals in relationships with the addicted individual.

Δ   Substance abuse harms family life, the economy, and public safety.

Δ   Addiction is a pattern of pathological, compulsive use of substances that can involve physiological dependence. Cardinal signs of addiction are tolerance and withdrawal. Denial is also a primary sign of addiction and may include defensiveness, lying about use, minimizing use, blaming or rationalizing use, and intellectualizing.

Δ   Alcohol, tobacco, and other drug abuse and addiction can cause multiple health problems, including low birth weight, congenital abnormalities, accidents, homicides, suicides, chronic diseases, and violence.

Δ   Recovery from substance addiction occurs over years and usually involves relapses. A strong support system, including 12-step programs and self-help groups for family members, is important.

Δ   Community health nurses are front-line health professionals who are able to assist those with addiction.

Δ   Alcohol Use

- Alcohol is the most commonly used substance in the United States. It is socially acceptable, as well as easily accessible.

- Alcohol is a depressant. Alcohol dulls the senses to outside stimulation and sedates the inhibitory centers in the brain.

- The direct effect of alcohol is determined by the blood alcohol level. The body processes alcohol dependent on several factors, including the size and weight of the drinker, gender (affects metabolism), carbonation (increases absorption), time elapsed during alcohol consumption, food in the stomach, and the drinker's emotional state. Alcohol is filtered by the liver at about 1 oz per hour. Excess alcohol that is not metabolized circulates in the blood and affects the central nervous system and the brain.

- People who frequently and consistently drink alcohol develop a **tolerance**, an increased requirement for alcohol to achieve the desired effect. When people continue to drink consistently, they can develop **blackouts**, which are times when they continue to appear to function but later cannot remember anything about those times.

- Withdrawal from alcohol begins commonly about 6 hr after cessation of drinking. It can manifest itself with irritability, tremors, nausea, vomiting, headaches, diaphoresis, anxiety, and sleep disturbances. Increased blood pressure and pulse may result, with pulse being the clearest indicator of possible delirium tremens or alcohol withdrawal delirium. The prompt use of benzodiazepines at the onset of symptoms can prevent the serious complication of delirium tremens. It is important to determine the last drink the client has taken in order to accurately assess for signs of withdrawal and delirium tremens.

Δ Tobacco Use

- Smoking is the most preventable cause of death in the United States, according to the Centers for Disease Control and Prevention.

- Nicotine is a stimulant that temporarily creates a feeling of alertness and energy. Repeated use to avoid the subsequent "down" that will follow this period of stimulation leads to a vicious cycle of use and physical dependence (withdrawal effects if not consumed).

- Tolerance to nicotine develops quickly.

- Cigarette smoking results in deep inhalation of smoke, which poses the greatest health risk (cancer, cardiovascular disease, respiratory disease); however, cigars, pipes, and smokeless tobacco increase the risk of cancers of the lips, mouth, and throat. Secondhand smoke poses considerable health risk (respiratory disease, lung cancer) to nonsmokers.

Δ Other Drugs

- Other stimulants include caffeine, amphetamines, and cocaine.

- Other depressants include barbiturates, benzodiazepines, opioids, and heroin.

- Hallucinogens (psychedelics) can produce euphoria, stimulation, and hallucinations. Some examples are lysergic acid diethylamide (LSD), phencyclidine (PCP), and MDMA (Ecstasy).

- Inhalants are volatile substances that are inhaled ("huffed"). Death may result from acute cardiac dysrhythmias or asphyxiation.

Δ Individual Assessment

- Establish rapport with the client. Pose questions in a matter-of-fact tone. Be nonjudgmental. Communicate that the purpose of questioning is because of the effects that different practices can have on an individual's health. Use the communication technique of normalizing when appropriate.

- Seek information about specific substances used, methods of use, and the quantity (e.g., packs, ounces) and frequency of use.

- Elicit information about consequences experienced (e.g., blackouts, overdoses, injuries to self/others, legal or social difficulties).

- Determine if the individual perceives a substance abuse problem.

- Discuss the individual's history of previous rehabilitation experiences.

- Gather family history of substance abuse and social exposure to other substance users.

- Some physical assessment findings include:

  ◊ Vital signs: Blood pressure, pulse, and temperature may be elevated, while respirations may be rapid, shallow, and depressed.

  ◊ Appearance: Individual may appear disheveled with an unsteady gait.

  ◊ Eyes: dilated or pinpoint pupils, redness, poor eye contact.

  ◊ Skin: diaphoretic, cool, clammy; needle track marks or spider angiomas may be visible.

  ◊ Nose: runny, congested, possibly red and cauliflower-shaped.

  ◊ Tremors: Fine or coarse tremors may be present.

Δ Strategies to Reduce Substance Abuse

- Primary prevention

  ◊ The focus is on inhibiting individuals from a first use and on preventing experimental users from progressing to chronic substance use or expansion to use of other drugs.

  ◊ Increase public awareness, particularly among young people, regarding the hazards and addictive qualities of substance abuse (e.g., public education campaigns, school education programs).

  ◊ Encourage development of life skills.

  ◊ Identify at-risk individuals and assist them to reduce sources of stress, including possible referral to social services to eliminate financial difficulties or other sources of stress.

- Secondary prevention

  ◊ The focus is on screening individuals for excessive substance use.

  ◊ Provide client education regarding interventions, including detoxification, medication therapy, and self-help groups.

  ◊ Family education and referrals assist families in dealing with abuse.

  ◊ Make referrals to develop new patterns of family interactions.

- Tertiary prevention

  ◊ The focus is on avoiding relapse of individuals who have already been treated for substance abuse.

  ◊ Assist the client to develop a plan to avoid high-risk situations and to enhance coping and lifestyle changes.

  ◊ Refer the client to community groups, such as Alcoholics Anonymous (AA) and Narcotics Anonymous (NA).

  ◊ Monitor pharmacological management.

  ◊ Provide emotional support to recovering abusers and their families, including positive reinforcement.

Mental Illness

Δ   Mental Illness Characteristics

- Occurs across the lifespan

- High risk of substance abuse

- High suicide risk

- Specific disorders

    ◊   Affective disorders (major depression, bipolar disorder)

    ◊   Anxiety disorders (panic, obsessive-compulsive, posttraumatic stress, phobias)

    ◊   Schizophrenia

    ◊   Dementia

    ◊   Conduct disorders

    ◊   Eating disorders

Δ   Factors Contributing to Mental Health of Aggregates

- Individual coping abilities

- Stressful life events (exposure to violence)

- Social events (recent divorce, separation, unemployment, bereavement)

- Chronic health problems

- Stigma associated with seeking mental health services

Δ   Primary Prevention

- Educate populations regarding mental health issues.

- Teach stress-reduction techniques.

- Provide parenting classes.

- Provide bereavement support.

- Promote protective factors (coping abilities) and risk factor reduction.

Δ   Secondary Prevention

- Screen to detect mental health disorders.

- Work directly with individuals, families, and groups through the formation of a therapeutic relationship.

- Conduct crisis intervention.

- Perform medication monitoring.

- Provide mental health interventions.

Δ Tertiary Prevention

- Make referrals to various groups of professionals, including support groups.

- Maintain the client's level of function to prevent relapse or frequent rehospitalization.

- Identify behavioral, environmental, and biological triggers that may lead to relapse.

- Assist the client in planning a regular lifestyle and minimizing sources of stress.

- Educate the client and family regarding medication side effects, potential interactions of medications, and alcohol use.

- Advocate for rehabilitation and recovery services.

Homelessness

Δ Homeless Population Characteristics

- Adults who are unemployed, earn low wages, or are migrant workers

- Female heads of household

- Families with children (fastest growing segment)

- Persons who are mentally ill (large segment)

- People who abuse alcohol or other substances

- Abandoned children

- Adolescent runaways

- Older adults with no one to care for them

- Vietnam War-era veterans

Δ Health Conditions of Homeless Populations

- Upper respiratory disorders

- Tuberculosis

- Skin disorders (e.g., athlete's foot) and infestations (e.g., scabies, lice)

- Alcoholism/drug abuse

- HIV/AIDS

- Assault and rape

- Mental illness

- Dental caries

- Hypothermia and heat-related illnesses

- Malnutrition

△ Primary Prevention

- The focus is on preventing individuals and families from becoming homeless by assisting them in eliminating factors that may contribute to homelessness.

- Refer those with underlying mental health disorders to therapy and counseling.

- Enhance parenting skills that may prevent young people from feeling the need to run away.

- Support major changes in societal structure, such as federal support for low-cost housing, increases in minimum wage, programs to train people with employable skills, and access to supportive services for those who are mentally and physically disabled.

△ Secondary Prevention

- The focus is on alleviating existing homelessness by making referrals for financial assistance, food supplements, and health services.

- Assist homeless clients in locating temporary shelter.

- If homeless shelters are not provided in the community, work with government officials to develop shelter programs.

- As shelters are an emergency resource, assist clients in finding ways to meet long-term shelter needs.

△ Tertiary Prevention

- Prevent recurrence of poverty, homelessness, and health problems that result in conditions of poverty and homelessness.

- Advocate and provide efforts toward political activity to provide needed services for people who are mentally ill and homeless.

- Make referrals for employee assistance and educational programs to allow clients who are homeless to eliminate the factors contributing to their homelessness.

Rural and Migrant Health

△ Health Status of Rural Residents

- Higher infant and maternal morbidity rates

- Higher rates of chronic illnesses (heart, lung, hypertension, cancer, diabetes mellitus) and motor vehicle crash-related injuries

- Higher health occupational risks, such as machinery accidents, skin cancer, and respiratory problems due to chemical exposure

- Higher rates of suicide

- High risk of trauma and injuries (falls, amputations, crush injuries, pesticide exposure)

- Less likely to seek medical care

Δ   Barriers to Health Care in Rural Areas

- Distance from services
- Lack of personal/public transportation
- Unpredictable weather and/or travel conditions
- Inability to pay for care/underinsured/uninsured
- Shortage of rural hospitals/health care providers

Δ   Health Problems of Migrant Workers

- Dental disease
- Tuberculosis
- HIV
- Depression and other mental health problems
- Domestic violence
- Lack of prenatal care
- Higher infant mortality rates

Δ   Issues in Migrant Health

- Poor and unsanitary working and housing conditions
- Less access to dental, mental health, and pharmacy services
- Inability to afford care
- Availability of services (distance, transportation, hours of service, health record tracking)
- Language (majority speak Spanish) and cultural aspects of health care

Δ   Primary Prevention

- Educate regarding measures to reduce exposure to pesticides.
- Teach regarding accident prevention measures.
- Provide prenatal care.
- Mobilize preventive services (e.g., dental, immunizations).

Δ   Secondary Prevention

- Screen for pesticide exposure.
- Screen for skin cancer.
- Screen for chronic preventable diseases.
- Screen for communicable diseases.

Δ   Tertiary Prevention

•   Treat for symptoms of pesticide exposure.

•   Mobilize primary care and emergency services.

Environmental Health

Δ   Environmental Risks

•   Toxins (lead, pesticides, mercury, air pollution, solvents, asbestos, radon)

•   Air pollution (ozone, carbon monoxide, particulate matter, nitrogen dioxide, sulfur dioxide, lead, aerosols, tobacco smoke)

•   Water pollution (wastes, erosion after mining or timbering, run-off from chemicals added to the soil)

Δ   Roles for Nurses in Environmental Health

•   Community involvement and public participation (organizing community participation in decisions, informing, facilitating discussions)

•   Individual and population risk assessment

•   Risk communication

•   Epidemiological investigations

•   Policy development

Δ   Assessment of Environmental Health

•   "I Prepare" model

◊   **I** = Investigate potential exposures

◊   **P** = Present work (exposures, use of personal protective equipment, location of material safety data sheets [MSDS], taking home exposures, trends)

◊   **R** = Residence (age of home, heating, recent remodeling, chemical storage, water)

◊   **E** = Environmental concerns (air, water, soil, industries in neighborhood, waste site or landfill nearby)

◊   **P** = Past work (exposures, farm work, military, volunteer, seasonal, length of work)

◊   **A** = Activities (hobbies, activities, gardening, fishing, hunting, soldering, melting, burning, eating, pesticides, alternative healing/ medicines)

◊   **R** = Referrals and resource (Environmental Protection Agency, Agency for Toxic Substances & Disease Registry, Association of Occupational and Environmental Clinics, MSDS, OSHA, local health department, environmental agency, poison control)

◊   **E** = Educate (risk reduction, prevention, follow-up)

- Key questions for environmental health history

    ◊ Housing: What is the location, age, and physical condition of residence, school, day care, or work site? Are lighting, ventilation, and heating/cooling systems adequate?

    ◊ What are the occupations of household members (current and past, longest-held jobs)?

    ◊ Is tobacco smoke present?

    ◊ Are there any recent home remodeling activities, such as the installation of new carpet or furniture or refinishing of furniture?

    ◊ What hobbies are done in the home?

    ◊ Is there any other recent exposure to chemicals or radiation?

    ◊ Are pets present in the home, and are they healthy?

    ◊ Has there been any lead exposure in old paint, crafts, leaded pottery, or dishes?

    ◊ What is the source and quality of the drinking water?

    ◊ How is sewage and waste disposed of in the home?

    ◊ Are there pesticides used around the home or garden? Is there any evidence of mold or fungi?

    ◊ Where do children play? Is there any hazardous play equipment or toys?

    ◊ Does the surrounding neighborhood present any hazards with closeness to highways or small businesses, such as dry cleaning, photo processing, industry, or auto repair?

△ *Healthy People 2010* Initiatives

- Reductions in:

    ◊ Proportion of persons exposed to air pollutants

    ◊ Toxic air emissions

    ◊ Waterborne disease outbreaks

    ◊ Per capita domestic water use

    ◊ Number of beach closings

    ◊ Potential human exposure to persistent chemical by decreasing fish-contaminated levels

    ◊ Pesticide exposures

    ◊ Amount of toxic pollutants released or used for energy recovery

    ◊ Indoor allergen levels

- Increases in:
    - ◊ Use of alternative modes of transportation to reduce motor-vehicle emissions
    - ◊ Nation's air quality
    - ◊ Proportion of persons served by community water systems who receive a supply of drinking water that meets Safe Drinking Water Act regulations
    - ◊ Proportion of rivers and lakes that are safe for fishing
    - ◊ Recycling of waste
- Eliminate elevated blood levels of lead in children.

Δ Primary Prevention

- The focus is on teaching individuals and populations to reduce environmental hazards.
- Advocate for safe air and water.
- Support programs for waste reduction and recycling.
- Advocate for waste reduction and effective waste management.

Δ Secondary Prevention

- The focus is on signs and symptoms of environmental exposures.
- Survey for health conditions that may be related to environmental and occupational exposures.
- Assess homes, schools, work sites, and the community for environmental hazards.
- Obtain environmental health histories for individuals.
- Screen children 6 months to 5 years old for blood lead levels.
- Monitor workers for levels of chemical exposures at job sites.

Δ Tertiary Prevention

- The focus is on minimizing disability and maximizing functional capacity.
- Become active in consumer and health-related organizations and legislation related to environmental health issues.
- Support cleanup of toxic waste sites and removal of other hazards.
- Refer homeowners to lead abatement resources.

Primary Reference:

Stanhope, M., & Lancaster, J. (2006). *Foundations of nursing in the community: Community-oriented practice* (2nd ed.). St. Louis, MO: Mosby.

Chapter 12: Special Community Needs

Application Exercises

Scenario: A community mental health nurse is conducting a depression screening within a community. During the screening, the nurse assesses a 40-year-old man who has been divorced for 6 months. His two children, ages 13 and 15, are now living with their mother. The children refuse to talk to or see him. He has lost 20 lb since the divorce and says he lacks motivation to get out of the house to do anything besides go to work. He reports that he has difficulty falling asleep at night. He says he does not want to be labeled as "weird" for seeing a psychiatrist for mental health concerns.

1. What factors may be adversely affecting the mental health of this client?

2. What level of prevention is appropriate for interventions with this client at the screening? What are some examples of interventions at this level?

Scenario: A 19-year-old college freshman is seen at a community-based clinic for a follow-up exam for a broken leg, lacerations, and contusions. His chart reveals that these injuries were caused when the car he was driving hit a tree. His blood alcohol level was 0.189% 3 hr after the incident. He reports that he had spent the previous evening at a friend's apartment and had consumed a couple of beers. On his way home, he missed a turn and hit a tree. He sums it up as "no big deal."

3. What questions should the nurse ask to assess if the client is at risk for substance abuse?

4. What level of prevention is appropriate when working with this client at the clinic? What are examples of interventions at this level?

5. A community health nurse is working in a rural community. The nurse is to plan screenings and client education based on issues that affect the health of the rural community. Identify the health promotion and disease prevention screenings and education interventions that should be planned.

Chapter 12: Special Community Needs

Application Exercises Answer Key

Scenario: A community mental health nurse is conducting a depression screening within a community. During the screening, the nurse assesses a 40-year-old man who has been divorced for 6 months. His two children, ages 13 and 15, are now living with their mother. The children refuse to talk to or see him. He has lost 20 lb since the divorce and says he lacks motivation to get out of the house to do anything besides go to work. He reports that he has difficulty falling asleep at night. He says he does not want to be labeled as "weird" for seeing a psychiatrist for mental health concerns.

1. What factors may be adversely affecting the mental health of this client?

   Recent divorce and children not interacting with him
   Perceived stigma associated with seeking mental health services

2. What level of prevention is appropriate for interventions with this client at the screening? What are some examples of interventions at this level?

   Secondary prevention is appropriate. Specifically, the client needs to be screened for a mental health disorder. Some examples of secondary prevention interventions include identification of the illness in need of treatment (assessment), formation of a therapeutic relationship, and referral to necessary community resources.

Scenario: A 19-year-old college freshman is seen at a community-based clinic for a follow-up exam for a broken leg, lacerations, and contusions. His chart reveals that these injuries were caused when the car he was driving hit a tree. His blood alcohol level was 0.189% 3 hr after the incident. He reports that he had spent the previous evening at a friend's apartment and had consumed a couple of beers. On his way home, he missed a turn and hit a tree. He sums it up as "no big deal."

3. What questions should the nurse ask to assess if the client is at risk for substance abuse?

Have you increased the amount of alcohol that you consume to obtain the effects that you used to have after a smaller amount of alcohol?
Do you have a persistent desire to use alcohol?
How often do you consume alcohol?
Has your frequency of alcohol consumption increased or decreased over the past month?
Have you missed classes or work because of use of alcohol?

4. What level of prevention is appropriate when working with this client at the clinic? What are examples of interventions at this level?

Secondary prevention is appropriate. Specifically, the client needs to be screened for a substance abuse problem. Some examples of secondary prevention interventions include:
Assess habits and history related to excessive alcohol consumption and use.
In a nonjudgmental way, educate the client about the effects of alcohol, risks of drinking and driving, and the importance of preventing another motor vehicle crash.
Explore the client's readiness and motivation to change his behavior.
Explore alternative activities and college programs for recreation.
If he chooses to make behavior changes, refer the client to a support group and/or counselor if necessary.
If he chooses not to make immediate changes, encourage him to follow up with another appointment and to think about a decision that would promote health.

5. A community health nurse is working in a rural community. The nurse is to plan screenings and client education based on issues that affect the health of the rural community. Identify the health promotion and disease prevention screenings and education interventions that should be planned.

Blood pressure
Nutrition
Diabetes mellitus
Cholesterol
Tobacco use
Alcohol use or abuse
Substance abuse
Responsible use of prescription and over-the-counter medications
Prenatal screenings and education
Immunizations for all ages
Cancer screenings (mammography, skin inspection, breast, testicular, Pap smears)
Safety and exposure education

Chapter 13:	Community Protection: Control of Communicable Diseases
	Contributor: Christine L. Vandenhouten, MSN, RN, CNOR

 Learning Objectives:

Δ   Discuss the modes of infectious disease transmission in relation to the prevention of the spread of those diseases.

Δ   Discuss the responsibility of the community health nurse in surveillance and reporting of infectious diseases.

Δ   Discuss the role of the community health nurse in promoting and providing immunizations.

Δ   Discuss the community health nurse's role in infectious disease control interventions (all three levels of prevention).

 Key Points

Δ   Worldwide, infectious diseases are responsible for the deaths of millions each year.

Δ   Most deaths are from pneumonia, diarrheal diseases, tuberculosis, malaria, measles, and HIV/AIDS.

Δ   Populations at risk for communicable disease include young children, older adults, immunosuppressed clients, intravenous drug users, and health care workers.

Δ   Routine immunizations for persons of various ages are recommended by the Centers for Disease Control and Prevention (CDC). Recommendations are according to ages and include schedules/guidelines for persons ages 0 to 6, 7 to 18, and 19 and up. The CDC Web site (*www.cdc.gov*) provides a quality resource for the most current information regarding immunization guidelines.

Modes of Transmission

Δ   Airborne (inhaled by a susceptible host)

- Measles

- Chickenpox

- Streptococcal infection

- Tuberculosis

- Pneumonia

- Influenza

Δ Foodborne (bacterial, viral, or parasitic infection of food)

- Salmonellosis

- Hepatitis A

- Trichinosis

- *Escherichia coli* (*E. coli*)

Δ Waterborne (fecal contamination of water)

- Cholera

- Typhoid fever

- *Giardia lamblia*

Δ Vector-borne (via a carrier such as a mosquito or tick)

- Lyme disease

- Rocky mountain spotted fever

- Malaria

Δ Direct Contact (skin-to-skin or contact with mucous membrane discharges)

- Sexually transmitted diseases (HIV, gonorrhea, syphilis, genital herpes, hepatitis B, C, and D)

- Infectious mononucleosis

- Impetigo, lice, scabies

Portals of Entry and Exit

Δ Portals of Entry

- Respiratory system

- Gastrointestinal tract

- Skin

- Mucous membranes

Δ Portals of Exit

- Respiratory system

- Feces

- Blood

- Semen/vaginal secretions

- Saliva

- Skin

Defense Mechanisms

Δ Natural Immunity (from the body's antigen antibody response)

Δ Artificial Immunity (through vaccination)

- Active (vaccination with live, killed, or toxoid)

- Passive (from antitoxin or antibodies)

Prevention and Control Measures for Communicable Diseases

Δ **Infectious Disease Surveillance**

- The community health nurse engages in infectious disease surveillance, which includes the systematic collection and analysis of data regarding infectious diseases.

- State law mandates which communicable diseases are reported to the CDC, and these vary by state. Some diseases included in the National Notifiable Diseases Surveillance System are:

    ◊ AIDS

    ◊ Anthrax

    ◊ Botulism

    ◊ Cholera

    ◊ Diphtheria

    ◊ Encephalitis

    ◊ Giardiasis

    ◊ Gonorrhea

    ◊ Hepatitis A-D

    ◊ Influenza activity

    ◊ Legionellosis/Legionnaires' disease

    ◊ Leprosy

    ◊ Lyme disease

    ◊ Malaria

    ◊ Meningococcal infections

◊ Mumps

◊ Pertussis

◊ Poliomyelitis

◊ Rabies

◊ Rocky Mountain spotted fever

◊ Rubella

◊ Rubeola (measles)

◊ Salmonellosis

◊ Shigellosis

◊ Severe acute respiratory syndrome-associated Coronavirus disease (SARS-CoV)

◊ Syphilis

◊ Smallpox

◊ Tetanus

◊ Toxic shock syndrome

◊ Trichinosis

◊ Tuberculosis

◊ Typhoid fever

◊ Vancomycin-resistant *Staphylococcus aureus* (VRSA)

◊ Varicella (chickenpox)

Healthy People 2010

Δ Goals Related to the Control of Communicable Diseases

• Reductions in:

◊ Indigenous cases of vaccine-preventable disease

◊ Invasive pneumococcal infections

◊ Meningococcal disease

◊ Lyme disease

◊ Tuberculosis

◊ Invasive early-onset Group B streptococcal disease

◊ Hospitalizations caused by peptic ulcer disease

◊ Number of courses of antibiotics for ear infections for young children

◊ Vaccine-associated adverse effects

- Increases in:

  ◊ Proportion of tuberculosis patients who complete curative therapy within 12 months

  ◊ Proportion of international travelers who receive recommended preventive services when traveling in areas of risk for select diseases, such as hepatitis A, malaria, and typhoid

  ◊ Effective vaccination coverage levels

Immunization

Δ The community health nurse plays a major role in increasing immunization coverage.

Δ Immunizations are often administered in community health settings, such as public health departments.

Δ The community health nurse often tracks immunization schedules of at-risk populations.

Δ The community health nurse must educate the community about the importance of immunizations.

Δ The community health nurse must stay up to date on current immunization schedule recommendations and appropriate precautions when administering immunizations.

Levels of Prevention

Δ **Primary Prevention**

- Prevent the occurrence of infectious disease.

- Educate the public regarding the need for immunizations, federal and state vaccination programs, and immunization laws such as the "no-shots, no school" legislation.

- Counsel clients traveling to other countries about protection from infectious diseases. Refer clients to the health department for information about mandatory immunizations.

- Educate the public regarding prevention of disease and ways to eliminate risk factors for exposure, such as handwashing, universal precautions, proper food handling and storage, and use of condoms.

Δ **Secondary Prevention**

- Early detection through screening and case finding is important.

- Refer suspected cases of communicable disease for diagnostic confirmation and epidemiologic reporting.

- Treat postexposure infections (e.g., hepatitis A, rabies).

- Quarantine when necessary.

Δ **Tertiary Prevention**

- Decrease complications and disabilities due to infectious diseases through treatment and rehabilitation.

- Monitor treatment compliance, including directly observed therapy.

- Prevent reinfection.

- Identify community resources.

Primary Reference:

Stanhope, M., & Lancaster, J. (2006). *Foundations of nursing in the community: Community-oriented practice* (2nd ed.). St. Louis, MO: Mosby.

Additional Resources:

For more information about communicable diseases, agents of bioterrorism, travel health information, and surveillance data, go to the Centers for Disease Control and Prevention Web site, *www.cdc.gov*.

Chapter 13: Community Protection: Control of Communicable Diseases

Application Exercises

1. Using resources such as the CDC Web site, identify specific measures to prevent or control the spread of infectious diseases for each of the following risks.

Handling and storage of food:

Exposure to ticks:

Exposure to at-risk water:

Head lice infestation:

Scenario: A client reports a 2-day history of headache, abdominal pain, diarrhea, and nausea. He states that his 4-year-old son has also experienced these symptoms. He also reports that his son recently purchased a pet turtle from the local pet store.

2. Based on the client's history and symptoms, what type of communicable disease should be suspected?

3. What type of precautions should this family take?

Scenario: An engineer from a major company is preparing to travel abroad to conduct business in a country located in the malaria belt.

4. Describe the transmission of malaria.

5. Identify measures the client can take to prevent becoming infected with this potentially fatal disease.

6. An older adult client asks why he has to receive the flu vaccine every year instead of every 10 years like the tetanus diphtheria vaccine. What is the appropriate explanation for the client's need for an annual influenza immunization?

Chapter 13: Community Protection: Control of Communicable Diseases

Application Exercises Answer Key

1. Using resources such as the CDC Web site, identify specific measures to prevent or control the spread of infectious diseases for each of the following risks.

Handling and storage of food:

Wash hands repeatedly.
Thoroughly cook food.
Consume cooked food immediately.
Store cooked food carefully.
Reheat cooked foods thoroughly.
Avoid contact between raw foods and cooked foods.
Keep all kitchen surfaces meticulously clean.
Protect food from insects, rodents, and other animals.
Use pure water.

Exposure to ticks:

Decrease tick populations.
Avoid tick-infested areas.
Wear protective clothing (long sleeves and long pants tucked into socks).
Use repellants.
Immediately inspect for and remove ticks when returning indoors.

Exposure to at-risk water:

Boil water for at least 1 min before use.
Consume bottled water or water purified with iodine or chlorine compounds.
Avoid ice (freezing does not inactivate agents.)
Choose coffee or tea made with boiled water, carbonated beverages without ice, beer, wine, or canned juices.

Head lice infestation:

Discourage sharing of combs and hats.
Use anti-lice (pediculicide) medications.
Remove nits from the head with a fine-toothed comb.
Wash linens and clothing in hot water (130° F) and dry on high setting for at least 20 min.

Scenario: A client reports a 2-day history of headache, abdominal pain, diarrhea, and nausea. He states that his 4-year-old son has also experienced these symptoms. He also reports that his son recently purchased a pet turtle from the local pet store.

2. Based on the client's history and symptoms, what type of communicable disease should be suspected?

Turtles are a possible source of Salmonella infections. It is possible that both the father and son are experiencing symptoms consistent with this type of infection.

3. What type of precautions should this family take?

Person-to-person transmission is possible, so all family members should be assessed for symptoms. As with any foodborne disease, it is important that the family practices good hand hygiene before and after preparing and consuming food, after toileting, and after handling pets. If the father's occupation involves food handling or patient care, he should be excluded from work until he is asymptomatic. If the son attends day care, he should be excluded until he is asymptomatic, as well.

Scenario: An engineer from a major company is preparing to travel abroad to conduct business in a country located in the malaria belt.

4. Describe the transmission of malaria.

Malaria is a potentially fatal illness transmitted via the bite of an infected anopheles mosquito.

5. Identify measures the client can take to prevent becoming infected with this potentially fatal disease.

No vaccine is available for this disease, and medication resistance is a problem in many malaria-endemic countries. The client should take a prescribed antimalarial medication, such as chloroquine or mefloquine, for 1 to 2 weeks before leaving and 4 to 6 weeks after he returns. Despite taking medications, some travelers will become infected and should seek health care if they develop symptoms consistent with malaria (fever and chills for up to 1 year after returning home).

6. An older adult client asks why he has to receive the flu vaccine every year instead of every 10 years like the tetanus diphtheria vaccine. What is the appropriate explanation for the client's need for an annual influenza immunization?

Influenza is a viral respiratory infection transmitted via airborne or direct contact with infected droplets. There are three strains of influenza virus: A, B, and C. Type A is the strain most often responsible for influenza outbreaks, and it has the most serious consequences. This influenza strain changes constantly through a process called antigenic drift. Types B and C have viral strains that are more stable than type A. Antigenic drift is responsible for regional outbreaks and yearly epidemics. Occasionally, a new subtype of the influenza A virus appears as a result of antigenic shift. As a result of the constant drift and potential shift in the influenza viral strains, preparation of the influenza vaccine takes place every year based on the prediction of the variant most likely to circulate. For this reason, it is important that older adults and persons with chronic diseases receive an annual influenza vaccine each year.

Chapter 14: Community Protection: Disaster Management/Response
Contributor: Rebecca Runge Cailor, MSN, RN, FNP-C

 Learning Objectives:

Δ   Identify and discuss the roles of the community health nurse in disaster planning and management, specifically in the disaster management phases of preparedness, response, and recovery.

Δ   Identify and discuss the roles of the community health nurse in preparing for and responding to bioterrorism.

 Key Points

Δ   A **disaster** is an event that causes human suffering and demands more resources than are available in the community. A disaster may be man-made or naturally occurring.

Δ   **Three Levels of Disaster Management**

•   Disaster preparedness

◊   This type of management includes preparedness for natural, man-made, or terrorist disasters.

◊   The Federal Response Plan is a government plan that includes the Federal Emergency Management Agency (FEMA), U.S. Public Health Service, Centers for Disease Control and Prevention (CDC), and other government agencies. The plan guides the coordination of efforts in response to a disaster.

◊   Predisaster planning should include identification and assessment of populations at risk. Populations at risk are those populations that have fewer resources or less of an ability to withstand and survive a disaster without physical harm. These populations tend to be physically isolated, disabled, or unable to access disaster services. Strategic emergency planning is necessary to prevent the loss of lives in susceptible populations.

◊   Disaster preparedness should include planning for the possibility of worldwide pandemics (e.g., WHO/HHS Pandemic Avian Influenza Plan of 2005).

◊ Setting up a communication protocol is an important part of disaster planning. The communication plan should provide for access to emergency agencies, such as the American Red Cross. This plan may be in-house, local, state-wide, or national, depending on the size of the disaster.

◊ Mass casualty drills are drills or mock disasters where personnel practice duties in a planned disaster scenario.

• Disaster response

◊ Different agencies are responsible for different levels of disaster response. They include FEMA, the Office of Emergency Management (OEM), and the American Red Cross. At the local level, hospitals, emergency departments, public health departments, mental health workers, and rescue personnel are responsible and have separate disaster duties.

◊ Disaster management response includes an initial assessment of how big of an area is affected. This includes how many people are affected, how many are injured or dead, how much fresh water and food is available, and areas of risk or sanitation problems. Lack of response was a major issue in the 2005 Hurricane Katrina, as the initial assessment of damage was underestimated along the southern coast and in the New Orleans area.

◊ Nursing roles during a disaster response include triaging victims with serious versus minor injuries, prioritizing care of victims, and transferring those requiring immediate attention to medical facilities. Triage includes freeing acute care beds by determining which clients can be discharged (e.g., those who are hospitalized for diagnosis or observation). Other roles include giving tetanus shots, first aid, and medical attention to victims.

• Disaster recovery

◊ Recovery is the length of time that it takes involved agencies to restore the economic and civil life of the community. At an individual level, it is the time it takes one to become a functioning person within a community after a disaster.

◊ Plague and sanitation controls are important aspects of disaster recovery. In the Pakistani-Indian earthquake of 2005, tetanus became epidemic due to the lack of vaccines, the remoteness of villages, the isolation of populations, and the number of infected wounds.

◊ Posttraumatic stress disorder (PTSD) and delayed stress reactions (DSR) are common during the aftermath of disasters and may affect both caregivers and victims.

◊ Nursing roles in disaster recovery include stress counseling, home health care, and reassessment of health care needs of the affected population.

Δ   Roles of Community Health Nurses in Disaster Management

- Participation in risk assessment includes asking the following questions:

  ◊   What are the populations at risk within the community?

  ◊   Have there been previous disasters, natural or man-made?

  ◊   What size of an area or population is likely to be affected in a worst-case scenario?

  ◊   What is the community disaster plan?

  ◊   What kind of warning system is in place?

  ◊   What type of disaster response teams (e.g., volunteers, nurses, health professionals, emergency medical technicians, firemen) are there in place?

  ◊   What kinds of resource facilities (e.g., hospitals, shelters, churches, food-storage facilities) are available in the event of a disaster?

  ◊   What type of evacuation measures (boat, motor vehicle, train) will be needed?

  ◊   What type of environmental dangers (e.g., chemical plants, sewage displacement) may be involved?

- Participation in community disaster planning includes:

  ◊   Developing a disaster response plan based on the most probable disaster threats.

  ◊   Identifying the community disaster warning system and communication center and learning how to access it.

  ◊   Identifying the first responders in the community disaster plan.

  ◊   Making a list of agencies that are available for the varying levels of disaster, both locally and nationally.

  ◊   Defining the nursing roles in first priority, second priority, and third priority triage.

  ◊   Identifying the specific roles of personnel involved in disaster response and the chain of command.

  ◊   Locating all equipment and supplies needed for disaster management, including Level III suits, infectious control items, medical supplies, food, and potable water. Replenish these regularly.

  ◊   Checking equipment (including evacuation vehicles) regularly to ensure proper operation.

  ◊   Evaluating the efficiency, response time, and safety of disaster drills, mass casualty drills, and disaster plans.

- Participation in community disaster response includes:

  ◊ Participating in community disaster plans.

  ◊ Activating the disaster management plan.

  ◊ Performing triage and directing disaster victims, evacuation, quarantine, and management of shelters.

  ◊ Assessing disaster victims and caretakers for posttraumatic stress disorder (PTSD) or delayed stress reactions, and giving them psychological treatment after the disaster.

- Participation in evaluation of community disaster response includes:

  ◊ Evaluating the area, effect, and level of the disaster.

  ◊ Creating ongoing assessment and surveillance reports.

  ◊ Evaluating the efficiency of the disaster response teams.

  ◊ Estimating the length of time for recovery of community services, such as electricity and running potable water.

Δ Bioterrorism

- Agents of bioterrorism

  ◊ Category A biological agents are the highest priority agents, posing a risk to national security because they are easily transmitted and have high mortality rates. Examples include smallpox (variola), botulinum toxin, anthrax, tularemia, hemorrhagic viral fevers, and plague.

  ◊ Category B biological agents are the second highest priority because they are moderately easy to disseminate and have moderate morbidity rates and low mortality rates. Examples include typhus and cholera.

  ◊ Category C biological agents are the third highest priority, comprising emerging pathogens that could be engineered in the future for mass dissemination because they are available, easy to produce, and/or have a potential for high morbidity and mortality rates. Examples include Nipah virus and hantavirus.

Incident	Signs and Symptoms	Treatment/Prevention
Inhalational anthrax	• Sore throat • Fever • Muscle aches • Severe dyspnea • Meningitis • Shock	• IV ciprofloxacin (Cipro)
Botulism	• Difficulty swallowing • Progressive weakness • Nausea, vomiting, and abdominal cramps • Difficulty breathing	• Airway management • Antitoxin • Elimination of toxin
Smallpox	• High fever • Fatigue • Severe headache • Rash (starts centrally and spreads outward) that turns to pus-filled lesions • Vomiting • Delirium • Excessive bleeding	• Treatment: no cure • Supportive care: hydration, pain medication, antipyretics • Prevention: vaccine (provides 10-year immunity)
Ebola	• Sore throat • Headache • High temperature • Nausea, vomiting, diarrhea • Internal and external bleeding • Shock	• Treatment: no cure • Supportive care: minimization of invasive procedures • Prevention: vaccine

- Delivery mechanisms for biochemical agents

    ◊ Direct contact (e.g., subcutaneous anthrax)

    ◊ Simple dispersal device (e.g., airborne or nuclear)

    ◊ Water and food contamination

    ◊ Droplet or blood contact

- Role of the community health nurse

    ◊ Participate in planning and preparation for immediate response to a bioterrorist event.

    ◊ Identify potential biological agents for bioterrorism.

    ◊ Survey for and report bioterrorism activity (usually to the local health department).

    ◊ Promptly participate in measures to contain and control the spread of infections resulting from bioterrorist activity.

- Assessment of bioterrorism threat
  - ◊ Is the population at risk for sudden high disease rates?
  - ◊ Is the vector that normally carries a specific disease available in the geographical area affected?
  - ◊ Is there a potential delivery system within the community?
- Recognition of a bioterrorism event
  - ◊ Is there a rapidly increasing disease incidence in a normally healthy population?
  - ◊ Is a disease occurring that is unusual for the area?
  - ◊ Is an endemic occurring at an unusual time? For example, is there an outbreak of influenza in the summer?
  - ◊ Are there large numbers of people dying rapidly with similar presenting symptoms?
  - ◊ Are there any individuals presenting with unusual symptoms?
  - ◊ Are there unusual numbers of dead or dying animals, unusual liquids/vapors/odors?
- Primary prevention
  - ◊ Preparation with bioterrorism drills, vaccines, and antibiotics for exposure prophylaxis
  - ◊ Bioterrorism planning
    - ° Design a bioterrorist response plan utilizing the most probable biochemical agent in the local area.
    - ° Assess and locate the local facilities that have Level I, Level II, Level III, and Level IV biosafety gear.
    - ° Identify the chain of command for reporting bioterrorist attacks.
    - ° Define the nursing roles in the event of a bioterrorist attack.
    - ° Set up protocols for different biosafety levels of infection control and containment.
- Secondary prevention
  - ◊ Early recognition
  - ◊ Activation of bioterrorism response plan in response to a bioterrorist event
  - ◊ Immediate implementation of infection control and containment measures, including decontamination, environmental disinfection, protective equipment, community education/notification, and quarantines

◊ Screening the population for exposure, assessing rates of infection, and administering vaccines as available

◊ Assisting with and educating the population regarding symptom identification and management (immunoglobulin, antiviral, antitoxins, and antibiotic therapy, depending on the agent)

◊ Monitoring mortality and morbidity

- Tertiary prevention

◊ Rehabilitation of survivors

◊ Monitoring medication regimens and referrals

◊ Evaluating the effectiveness and timeliness of the bioterrorism plan

Primary Reference:

Stanhope, M., & Lancaster, J. (2006). *Foundations of nursing in the community: Community-oriented practice* (2nd ed.). St. Louis, MO: Mosby.

Additional Resources:

Centers for Disease Control and Protection. (n.d.). *Bioterrorism agents/diseases (by category)*. Retrieved March 23, 2007, from http://www.bt.cdc.gov/agent/agentlist-category.asp#c

For more information, go to the CDC site, *www.cdc.gov*, and the FEMA Web site, *www.fema.gov*.

Chapter 14: Community Protection: Disaster Management/Response

Application Exercises

1. A community health nurse is a first responder to a bombing incident and is assigned to the triage area. Which of the following victims with life-threatening injuries should be given the highest priority?

    A. The most seriously injured victims

    B. Victims with the highest probability for survival

    C. Victims needing immediate transportation to a trauma center

    D. Victims at the highest risk for systemic complications

2. In the event of a smallpox threat, would individuals who were vaccinated against smallpox prior to 1972 (when smallpox was eradicated in the U.S.) need to be vaccinated? Why or why not?

Scenario: A community health nurse is working in a county clinic where five cases of avian influenza virus have been confirmed (positive blood samples). The public health department has been notified.

---

3. What should be the community health nurse's next action?

4. What phase of disaster management is this?

Scenario: A nurse is working in an emergency department within a large metropolitan area. There is a minor explosion in a high-rise building downtown. Three hours later, the emergency department is flooded with clients from this high-rise building, who are presenting with problems breathing and flu-like symptoms. The building has no known chemicals or asbestos in the offices that would explain these symptoms.

5. Name two organisms that may be causative factors in respiratory failure as bioterrorist agents.

6. To whom should the emergency department nurse report the suspected bioterrorism attack?

7. The public health department is on site and the bioterrorism defense plan has been activated. The downtown area and hospital staff are now quarantined by local law enforcement agencies, the National Guard, and CDC officials. The agent has been identified as respiratory inhaled anthrax. Into what category of biological agent does anthrax fit?

Chapter 14: Community Protection: Disaster Management/Response

Application Exercises Answer Key

1. A community health nurse is a first responder to a bombing incident and is assigned to the triage area. Which of the following victims with life-threatening injuries should be given the highest priority?

    A. The most seriously injured victims

    B. Victims with the highest probability for survival

    C. Victims needing immediate transportation to a trauma center

    D. Victims at the highest risk for systemic complications

In situations in which health resources are limited, a client's likelihood of survival must be the determinant of priority assignment. Community health nurses may be required to assist in deciding which clients to treat based on an assessment of each client's likelihood of survival with intervention. In these tough circumstances, priority is given to clients who have a reasonable chance of survival with prompt intervention. Clients who have a limited likelihood of survival even with intense intervention are assigned the lowest priority.

2. In the event of a smallpox threat, would individuals who were vaccinated against smallpox prior to 1972 (when smallpox was eradicated in the U.S.) need to be vaccinated? Why or why not?

Yes: The smallpox vaccination provides only 10 years of immunity.

Scenario: A community health nurse is working in a county clinic where five cases of avian influenza virus have been confirmed (positive blood samples). The public health department has been notified.

---

3. What should be the community health nurse's next action?

Priority should be given to containing the initial outbreak of a potential pandemic. Appropriate actions prior to the arrival of the public health department officials include initiating a quarantine of those inside the clinic (including staff) and closure of the clinic. When public health department officials arrive, they will take blood samples for avian influenza DNA testing from the staff. A reportable communicable disease form needs to be completed for each of the confirmed cases. The public health department may involve the law enforcement agency to quarantine others as needed.

4. What phase of disaster management is this?

This is the disaster response phase. This phase involves activation of the disaster management plan, triage and management of disaster victims, evacuation, quarantine, and management of shelters as needed depending upon the level of disaster.

Scenario: A nurse is working in an emergency department within a large metropolitan area. There is a minor explosion in a high-rise building downtown. Three hours later, the emergency department is flooded with clients from this high-rise building, who are presenting with problems breathing and flu-like symptoms. The building has no known chemicals or asbestos in the offices that would explain these symptoms.

5. Name two organisms that may be causative factors in respiratory failure as bioterrorist agents.

There are various pneumonia-capable agents. The three most common are respiratory anthrax, tularemia, and bubonic plague.

6. To whom should the emergency department nurse report the suspected bioterrorism attack?

The public health department

7. The public health department is on site and the bioterrorism defense plan has been activated. The downtown area and hospital staff are now quarantined by local law enforcement agencies, the National Guard, and CDC officials. The agent has been identified as respiratory inhaled anthrax. Into what category of biological agent does anthrax fit?

Category A biological agents pose a high priority risk to national security, are easily transmitted, and have high mortality rates. Examples include smallpox (variola), botulinum toxin, anthrax, tularemia, hemorrhagic viral fevers, and plague.